Law and Economics

This book examines the contemporary significance of the Law and Economics movement.

Drawing on anthropology, sociology, political economy, and ethics, the book traces the influence of lawyer-economists in developing and operationalizing key ideas—for instance human capital and structural adjustment—that have come to be grouped under the heading of "neoliberalism". It then examines how these ideas are tied to global environmental harm and to wealth inequality. Largely because of such ties, sociolegal studies tend to dismiss economic thought. This book, however, forges a path between economic and sociolegal approaches. Discussing thinkers such as Foucault and Polanyi, Calabresi and Sunstein, it demonstrates both the possibilities and limitations inherent in economistic approaches to law. Bringing together disparate and sometimes conflicting literatures, the book thereby eschews disciplinary taboos in the name of a creative, sympathetic, and critical rereading of the key ideas of Law and Economics.

This book will be of interest to students and researchers in sociolegal studies, anthropology, sociology, and economics.

Riaz Tejani is Associate Professor of Business Ethics at the University of Redlands, California, USA.

Part of the NEW TRAJECTORIES IN LAW series

Series Editors

Adam Gearey, Birkbeck College, University of London
Prabha Kotiswaran, Kings College London
Colin Perrin, Commissioning Editor, Routledge
Mariana Valverde, University of Toronto

For information about the series and details of previous and forthcoming titles, see https://www.routledge.com/New-Trajectories-in-Law/book-series/NTL

a GlassHouse Book

Law and Economics

New Trajectories in Law

Riaz Tejani

Routledge
Taylor & Francis Group
a GlassHouse Book

First published 2023
by Routledge
4 Park Square, Milton Park, Abingdon, Oxon OX14 4RN

and by Routledge
605 Third Avenue, New York, NY 10158

Routledge is an imprint of the Taylor & Francis Group, an informa business

a GlassHouse book

British Library Cataloguing-in-Publication Data
A catalogue record for this book is available from the British Library

Library of Congress Cataloging-in-Publication Data
Names: Tejani, Riaz, 1977-author.
Title: Law and economics: new trajectories in law/Riaz Tejani.
Description: Abingdon, Oxon [UK]; New York, NY: Routledge, 2023. |
Series: New trajectories in law | Includes bibliographical references and index.
Identifiers: LCCN 2023014590 (print) | LCCN 2023014591 (ebook) |
ISBN 9781032396590 (hardback) | ISBN 9781032396606 (paperback) |
ISBN 9781003350767 (ebook)
Subjects: LCSH: Law and economics. | Globalization–Economic aspects.
Classification: LCC K487.E3 T457 2023 (print) | LCC K487.E3 (ebook) |
DDC 343.07–dc23/eng/20230519
LC record available at https://lccn.loc.gov/2023014590
LC ebook record available at https://lccn.loc.gov/2023014591

ISBN: 978-1-032-39659-0 (hbk)
ISBN: 978-1-032-39660-6 (pbk)
ISBN: 978-1-003-35076-7 (ebk)

DOI: 10.4324/9781003350767

Typeset in Sabon
by Deanta Global Publishing Services, Chennai, India

For Farhad and Zarin

Contents

Figures

Acknowledgments

This book is a critical survey of Law and Economics from the perspective of an economic and social anthropologist of law. I could not, therefore, have written it without talking to many people, and getting to know the "subfield", "community", or "movement" firsthand on numerous occasions. While this is not a social scientific (e.g., ethnographic) study of Law and Economics, it is a critical introduction to the field based on substantial bibliographic research and supplemented by dialogues with generous people inside and outside the field.

With that, I thank members of the American Law and Economics community for sharing their insights with me. Notably, Marc Abramowicz, Ian Ayres, Guido Calabresi, Jacob Goldin, Dan Klerman, Mark Lemley, Zach Liscow, Jonathan Masur, Eric Posner, Susan Rose-Ackerman, Robert Scott, Ilya Somin, Eric Talley, Kip Viscusi, and Kathy Zeiler provided substantial guidance on many of the questions pursued in this text.

I also thank colleagues in the Law and Society community who have shared critical insights about the Law–Economics–Society nexus with me over the years—their keen observations shaped this text immeasurably. This includes Deepa Das Acevedo, Paul Baumgardner, Leo Coleman, Laurie Edelman, Matthew Erie, Bryant Garth, Carol Greenhouse, Deborah Hensler, Greg Marks Beth Mertz, Sonia Rao, Justin Richland, and Matt Shaw among many others.

My colleagues at the University of Redlands, Carlo Carrascoso, Allison Fraiberg, and Denise MacNeil, have been a perennial source of support over the past four years, as has Dean Thomas Horan.

And finally, I thank my family, Kari, Macee, Aina, Milo, and Henri, for supporting my research and writing with seemingly endless patience and good cheer, and for challenging me to articulate my ideas with maximum clarity—something easily forgotten inside academic bubbles.

It is a distinct privilege to have had input from all these individuals. This book tries carefully to honor those investments, and any lapses in doing so are mine to own.

Introduction

Law and Economics Everywhere?

Introduction

Imagine if you were a world leader and Earth was faced with the threat of a deadly viral pandemic. Who would you call to prepare a response? It might make sense to assemble any number of national security experts, medical scientists, bioethicists, or epidemiologists. Together, they could paint a clear picture of the coming security risks, viral mutations, resource scarcities, and population immunity. But what about *lawyers*? Would you bother to call one, and, if so, what might they have to say? Recent history has an illustration.

As the COVID-19 pandemic began to hit Europe and North America, people were understandably scared. Previously, social connectedness had grown into a cultural phenomenon evidenced by the success of hot new "sharing economy" firms such as WeWork, Uber, and Airbnb. Now, even before the science of the virus was understood, connectedness and sharing looked like two of the greatest dangers to human survival. Friends were now a threat, and the panic this created led to a near-halt in commercial activity. Businesses suffered, and the stock market shuddered. Then a lawyer *was* consulted, but not just any lawyer: a lawyer-economist.

In March of that year, advisors in the U.S. President's inner circle found an article by the Law and Economics expert Richard Epstein, which took a very optimistic view of the long-term outlook. "In the United States", Epstein wrote, "if the total death toll increases at about the same rate, the current 67 deaths should translate into about 500 deaths at the end".[1] Unfortunately, this number was easily surpassed a week later (Worldometer 2022). The Hoover Institution, which

---

1 This quote of the original is taken from a subsequent interview (Chotiner 2020) which reproduced the original excerpt because the Hoover Institution changed the online version to reflect the belatedly revised estimate.

DOI: 10.4324/9781003350767-1

published the initial piece, revised the figure to 5,000 the next day (Epstein 2020a), and then again, five days later, Epstein projected as many as 40,000 deaths in a related interview with *The New Yorker* (Chotiner 2020). If this now sounds a bit like someone stabbing in the dark, it was—albeit with flawed mathematical models offered in support. The actual number of COVID-19 deaths reached an unthinkable 1 million in the United States by June of 2022 (New York Times 2022). At the early stages, few could have known how such a complex threat would unfold. And yet the incentives for claiming to know were quite high: national attention and high-level government interest—both of which Epstein received before the inevitable wave of public criticism that followed. Indeed, journalists have said that it was *his* article the White House relied upon most in its initial decision to take nearly no action (Chotiner 2020), a decision that almost certainly led to more deaths than necessary.

All of this raised one very important question: if a lawyer-economist could do little better than you or I at forecasting the public health crisis, why was one consulted and trusted in the first place? The answer lies at the heart of this book and why you might continue reading it. Lawyer-economists, and their field, Law and Economics, have reached a level of influence rarely seen among academics in modern history. By this, I mean that a single university-based, academic discipline has not often been so influential for so long. In the wake of World War II, many academics in the United States and Europe were asked to assist with the social, economic, and political reconstruction of Europe (see e.g., Ferri 2008; Leffler 1988). Yet, those efforts harnessed expertise from many different disciplines: anthropology, sociology, economics, and political science among others. In this case, lawyer-economists—most with high-level training in law and basic competence in economics—have risen to prominence to sit on Courts of Appeal, run government agencies, and lead powerful think tanks in surprisingly high numbers. Put otherwise, a field of this size has rarely gained such a capacity to influence social and political life. Whether or not this is a good thing, it certainly demands our curiosity.

Like other scientists, economists are an esoteric "knowledge community" with unique ways of seeing the world and a range of diverse methods and goals. Lawyers, meanwhile, are more commonly known to the general public by way of popular culture (e.g., there's really no economist version of John Grisham) and their sheer visibility in the population; the United States, for example, is home to 1.3 million attorneys as of 2021 (ABA 2021). That is roughly one lawyer for every 250 residents—more than any other country on Earth. Lawyers tend to be rule-oriented and keen interpreters of text. Yet for reasons explained throughout this book, neither economists nor lawyers alone have achieved as much success advancing a coherent policy agenda as their hybrid kin, the lawyer-economists. Both economics and law are powerful disciplines separately, but something distinct arises when you combine them. Law and Economics merges the rule-centered authoritativeness of the legal profession with the predictive, scientistic approach to human preferences and behaviors espoused by mainstream economics.[2] The combination of rule development and outcome predictability create both an approach and a community that have garnered significant acceptance among institutions of government, business, and academia. And yet, that approach and community do not sit *outside* wider contemporary social life. They and their success are social phenomena unto themselves; they have shaped our world in ways whose understanding requires that we learn about Law and Economics *in a social and cultural perspective.*

Supporting that idea, this book first highlights key subjects, themes, and assumptions inherent in the Law and Economics worldview, and presents some of the criticisms lodged by social science and humanities writers. Next, it describes specific ways in which Law and Economics has influenced the main Western legal subject areas: torts, contracts, property, business law, criminal, and administrative law. The book then ventures back in time to explain how Law and Economics arose in and changed the legal landscape, and then follows this with some comparative perspective—asking how the subfield has influenced certain legal systems around the world. It concludes with a summary discussion about where Law and Economics fits among broader global trends toward market economy, individualized responsibility, and wide-ranging contractions of government power. The concluding question it considers is whether and how Law and Economics is connected to market fundamentalism, or *neoliberalism*—the widespread belief that free exchange is the best hope for human prosperity and its distribution around the world today. This is a lot to cover. And yet, by homing in on vital concepts and developments, and by sparing much of the technical minutiae, it offers a readable account of the "who, what, when, where, and why" contributing to the current gaps between Law and Economics, its neighboring fields, and general public awareness. By extension, it suggests a plausible roadmap for bridging these gaps as well.

And who might be interested in building such a bridge? This book is aimed at students, scholars, journalists and practitioners interested in the state of legal knowledge in our contemporary world. How does law

---

2 This follows a very strong thread in the work of Milton Friedman who believed all good theory, especially in economics, must be predictive (see Ebenstein 2007).

interact with economic behavior? What motivates court decisions that prioritize business over social interests? And why has it become more difficult to reach consensus about what is "good" for us as a society? All of these questions come into focus when we bring law, economics, and society into the same field of vision.

Yet, there are also some noteworthy reasons for not bringing these fields into dialogue. Law and Economics and Sociolegal Studies—the name for broader social science and humanities research into law—have long viewed one another as professional rivals, and at odds about such basic premises as their methods for studying people, the way people behave under law, and the ethics that govern how law and policy should treat social realities. But, if we step back from precious core beliefs, these differences create a useful "discomfort" that leads to more rigorous thinking—an opportunity to challenge tacit knowledge and accepted wisdoms against those who approach the world differently. Academic communities have always struggled with this; with the tension between settling into accepted canons—*paradigms* in the language of Thomas Kuhn (2012)—and the ongoing push to disrupt those with something new or groundbreaking. I do not claim to offer anything like a paradigm shift in this short text. But I do believe examining Law and Economics with social science and humanities tools moves us closer to a complete picture of the way law operates in the world. And as the next section describes, Law and Economics has impacted certain aspects of that world more so than others.

Impact Zones

One of the key tenets of lawyer-economists—influenced by the famous Chicago School of economic thought—has been that markets are better than governments in "deciding" what is best for society (see Ebenstein 2007; Duxbury 1995). I use scare quotes there because a singular "decision" is purposely avoided—who would make that anyway?—and it is rather the aggregate decisions of thousands or millions of people that presumably result in collective choices about scarce resources or debatable values. Hence, we sometimes hear them say, "the market knows best".

For this reason, one of the earliest areas touched by Law and Economics was *regulatory* law. This refers to the body of rules and opinions surrounding federal and state regulatory agencies set up under the executive branches of each. Environmental protection, communications, air and ground transportation, and securities exchanges all fall under the control of such agencies. Initially, the first experts who saw law as a means to achieve economic objectives were antitrust attorneys working for the United States Department of Justice (D.O.J.) just after the Great

Depression. Those lawyers had as their job the enforcement of New Deal–era rules against monopolies and trusts—structures of collusion between firms in large, essential industries such as energy and transportation. Richard Posner, the figure most cited as a founder of Law and Economics, was an antitrust lawyer with the D.O.J. in his early professional days (Teles 2008). At the time, both lawyers and economists alike, still reeling from the Depression, largely accepted the prevailing wisdom taught by the English economist John Maynard Keynes that governments *must* step in to control interest rates and to stimulate national economies during predictable contractions that occur between economic growth cycles (Ebenstein 2007). But, as first-generation lawyer-economists grew older, and as the Cold War with the Soviet Union gave rise to deep suspicions about communism and socialism, strong government controls set up under the New Deal received greater criticism among certain economists. Above all, they came to be seen as a threat toward individual freedom. University of Chicago economist Milton Friedman would later pose the biggest challenge to Keynes by arguing that poor monetary policy, not unregulated markets, had been the primary cause of the Depression (Ebenstein 2007).

For economists, the virtue of markets is open competition. Whereas the early antitrust lawyers were concerned with large-firm monopolies in specific markets, the early lawyer-economists came to view strong regulatory law as anticompetitive. This followed the observation of another Chicago economist, George Stigler, that certain firms and professional associations often favor regulations that limit competitors and create more opportunity for themselves (Wheelan 2010, 91). One of the strongest signs that this view was later embraced can be seen in U.S. President Ronald Reagan's executive order 12291. Signed in 1981, 12291 says that the creation of new regulations by federal agencies must be accompanied by a "cost–benefit analysis" showing that the new rule or rules will provide a net economic benefit to the public. Since 1981, therefore, all new regulatory law has been subject to one of the key principles behind Law and Economics—a principle that rests upon a consequentialist view of ethics in society.

Tax law is a second area that has been greatly shaped by lawyer-economists. This group has been host to some very high-profile libertarian scholars and public intellectuals—writers who believe the proper role of government is to stay out of business and domestic activities. Professor Richard Epstein, described above, is one such writer, but there are many more to speak of. An early premise for such thinkers was that the law should work in the service of minimizing corporate and private tax burdens. This would be further consistent with the belief that expenditures on the part of government should remain selective to avoid interference with "natural" markets. If government spending remains low, then government revenues (e.g., taxes) can remain low and people will be freer to save or spend on projects *they* consider worthwhile. This builds on the work of some who argued low taxes allow greater individual spending such that governments will see *more* rather than less revenue in the long run (Wheelan 2010, 96).

But a new generation of lawyer-economists has taken a different position. For writers such as Zachary Liscow, the tax code is a site at which lawyers and economists may be able to combat widespread inequality. Looking beyond conventional wisdom about "progressive taxation"—which holds that the rich should pay more than the poor—Liscow and others see tax credits as an effective way to get money into the hands of people who need it most for reasons that may be of greater social value than what "trickle down" economists once proposed (Liscow 2022). This approach looks at strategies such as tax credits as a form of incentive, a way of convincing people to do or refrain from doing something. Incentives play a major role in the way Law and Economics conceptualizes solutions to large socio-economic problems.

Business law is a third major area impacted by lawyer-economists. This may seem obvious at first since business and economics *seem* to sit on two sides of the same coin. But it is less so if we reflect on the definitions of each, and the work that has gone into making these two fields nearly synonymous. Economics is the study of production, consumption, and distribution of goods and services in a society or community. Business is the practice of producing certain goods or services that add *value* to others' commercial activity or private lives, and the selling of those goods or services *for profit*. They may require understandings of one another, but they are far from synonymous. Economics takes into account both for-profit and non-profit activities—including especially a place for what Guido Calabresi has called "merit goods", or the types of goods a society has deemed to maintain *beyond* the realm of marketization and profit (2016). Health, love, and education are all to varying degrees treated this way; there may be private and for-profit ways to distribute or acquire each, but we tend to frown upon taking them away from someone without the ability to pay. Indeed, in certain cases such as love, Calabresi has pointed out, the expectation of payment *destroys* the good itself (2016). But what has brought these two subjects—business and economics—into such close relationship?

It is the vigorous embrace of markets as the primary means for distributing wealth in our society that best explains the marriage of business and economics. Numerous law schools around the world host some type of center for Law and Economics research. Many host research centers for Business Law. A handful have omitted the distinction entirely and combined these into one. The idea is that, in Western capitalist societies, the market solution to distributive justice—and therefore all the laws and regulations in place to secure markets from interference—assumes that people are motivated by the *will to profit*. Business, under that viewpoint, becomes the engine of economics, and Law and Economics has as much to do with regulation and taxes as it does about rules that stimulate business activity in the first place.

Policing and criminal justice form a fourth major area where lawyer-economists have been especially active. In some ways, this is connected to observations above about taxation. Both policing and criminal justice are heretofore public functions financed by taxation. The majority of lawyer-economists have held that—much like smaller government—lower taxes are better than higher because they allow individuals to spend on services *they* deem valuable. The way to lower taxes is to minimize government spending, which can be achieved by eliminating key services or by making those run more efficiently. Law and Economics experts have written widely about the efficient use of resources in law enforcement raising questions such as "how many extra police per capita are necessary before the resulting crime reductions cease to outweigh the costs?" And they have debated the benefits of private versus public prisons, asking, "if a government monopoly spends a certain amount to house each prisoner per year, how much may be saved by privatizing prisons to allow competition between firms?"

From one vantage point these questions are less about law than they are about administration and budgeting. How many police to employ is not a question about what the criminal law should prohibit or allow. Whether prisons should be run by a corporation is not itself a question about how long mandatory sentences should be. And yet, the efficiency of our public legal institutions is only one way of judging their effectiveness. Other ways might include public perceptions of safety, or of justice in society. So the Law and Economics approach to policing and prisons is a statement about what matters in the domain of public law, and how much justice or injustice, safety or unsafety, to tolerate in society. This evaluation of legal institutions and processes on the basis of efficiency, rather than public satisfaction, has been a key contribution of Law and Economics. But, as one would expect, it has many critics.

Along with the application of efficiency standards to regulatory, tax, business, and criminal law institutions, a similar scrutiny has been applied to social welfare programs. Welfare is an important term in Law and Economics with two important meanings, so it deserves some explaining. First, to most working adults, "welfare" refers to the public assistance programs long offered by many Western governments to ensure the survival of the poorest of their citizens. It can take the form of a direct income subvention to individuals, or a distribution of food or housing vouchers, or an offer of free public healthcare services. After the 1960s—in which the U.S. President Lyndon Johnson had declared a "war on poverty" and proposed a series of programs known as the "Great Society"—the United States federal government erected or revamped a series of agencies to ensure the poorest in the society had access to food, healthcare, housing, and even legal counsel. Republican President Richard Nixon even helped to expand some of these programs in an era when political party affiliation was not synonymous with fiscal spending approaches. But, by the late 1970s, the United States entered a period of intense "stagflation", and the world economy was significantly hampered by energy shortages and resulting supply chain issues. Incoming U.S. President Ronald Reagan—in many ways adopting the rhetoric of an earlier politician, Barry Goldwater—campaigned on a theory that "small government" was the key to tackling the problems of the day. This approach rested greatly on the economic theories of Milton Friedman and Frederick Von Hayek—both Chicago School academics with strong ties to the lawyer-economists of the time. For Reagan, small government did not mean a reduced military budget; it meant the key social programs such as welfare, food stamps, and public housing, needed to be minimized in favor of market solutions to the problems of inequality. Welfare, the conservative economists such as Friedman told him, artificially inflated prices and encouraged the poor to avoid finding work (Ebenstein 2007).

Income Gains Widely Shared in Early Postwar Decades — But Not Since Then

Real family income between 1947 and 2018, as a percentage of 1973 level

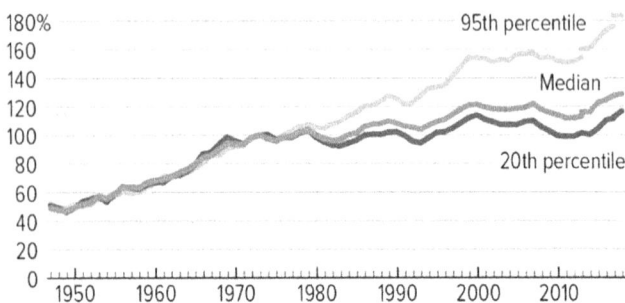

Note: Breaks indicate implementation of a redesigned questionnaire (2013) and an updated data processing system (2017).

Source: CBPP calculations based on U.S. Census Bureau Data

CENTER ON BUDGET AND POLICY PRIORITIES | CBPP.ORG

Figure 0.1 U.S. family income inequality growth between 1947 and 2018.

Note inflection point in 1981, the year President Reagan took office.

Source: CBPP.org

But second, "welfare", to lawyer-economists, can refer to the well-being or utility of a community. This is a term reaching far back in economic theory to the neoclassical writers Bentham, Mill, and Smith, and is sometimes expressed as "social welfare" or "the general welfare". So far, it would seem the two senses of "welfare"—government assistance and collective well-being—are closely related. Where they diverge, however, becomes apparent after asking the question of *who* should get the benefit of increasing "social welfare". Should it be the poor, the rich, both equally, or both unequally? While recent lawyer-economists have grown concerned that it should be "both" on some level, traditional Law and Economics did not greatly concern itself with this dilemma. The term *welfare* to those experts traditionally just meant the well-being of a community, and the role of distribution was best left up to open markets protected from outside controls. Believers in this approach, it turns out, were very close to the Reagan Administration (Baumgardner 2019) and they helped advise its policies of reducing taxes and expenditures for welfare programs in ways that remain visible to this day. And lest we come away thinking that this was merely a partisan effort—the result of Republican control over policy—we must remember that later presidents Clinton and Obama both embraced much of the same logic to administering social programs.

Finally, and relatedly, global finance and development has been another key area where Law and Economics has shaped the world around us. I group these together as one because the past 30 years have taught us that they are linked. It was previously understood that unequal development among nations of the world was a function of their histories: some had been colonies held for wealth extraction, and some had been metropoles to which extracted wealth had been sent, deposited, and invested. Still others served as waystations for global networks such as the "triangle trade" in slaves and sugar connecting Africa, the Americas, and Europe (Linebaugh and Rediker 2000). These accounts of underdevelopment are accurate. And yet, their persisting relevance is largely also the result of ongoing dynamics in the global financial markets, as well as international approaches to investment and trade. In other words, whether small countries in West Africa today have clean water, or usable Internet, may be as much the result of colonialism as it is the result of foreign direct investment. Therefore, the policies and legal institutions erected in each country, not to mention the establishment of a global legal order overseeing financial transactions and agreements, has direct impact on whether or not less-developed nations of the world have been able to, or are now able to, participate in the global economy. Put more concretely, those high-level institutions and approaches can determine whether people on the ground survive or flourish around the world. Lawyer-economists now play a significant role in shaping global finance and development. The most obvious example can be seen in the practices of the World Bank, the International Monetary Fund, and the World Trade Organization described in more detail in Chapter 3. These international financial institutions (IFIs) have for several decades stipulated that developing countries must undergo legal reforms to establish and protect open markets while moving away from state ownership. Perhaps not surprisingly, these reforms often benefit Western business firms—which have engaged in international operations for decades—while disadvantaging domestic firms that have only just begun to engage in global exporting. They also have helped boost the careers of domestic political figures more welcoming of foreign firms, and alternatively inspired political counter-movements against global market participation.

The preceding pages offered a quick glimpse into some of the key ways Law and Economics has, in recent decades, influenced law to shape social and political life in the United States and abroad. They establish the considerable importance of understanding the subfield, what it stands for, and how its experts think about solving problems. The following chapters of this book revisit those developments in greater detail. Before getting there, the next few sections of this introduction will consider some of the important themes that have preoccupied lawyer-economists and key questions raised by those themes.

Recurring Themes

Lawyer-economists are a diverse and evolving group. Admittedly, even to most I have spoken with, lawyer-economists are still predominantly white and male—much like professional Economics and Law practitioners separately. But at a certain level of specificity, notable differences can be found among members as to political persuasion, attitudes about government, and concern for social problems. Nevertheless, key common themes have emerged over the roughly 100 years in which this field has emerged and grown. This section introduces those and organizes them into themes of ethical, political-economic, psychological, sociological, and legal content.

Ethical

To be a lawyer-economist is typically to believe in a *consequentialist* ethical worldview—a view that evaluates right versus wrong on the basis of the results achieved by any given decision. Consequentialism is a major school of thought in Western moral philosophy, and it gave rise in 18th-century England to the more well-known substrand of *utilitarianism*. This approach still views consequences as paramount to decision-making, but it evaluates them for their "utility". Classically, to the original utilitarians Jeremy Bentham and John Stuart Mill, *utility* referred to pleasure or enjoyment—in other words the absence of pain (Posner 1981, 48). In a world where justifications for "right versus wrong" can vary wildly by culture, religion, and geography, utility seemed like a grounded, observable standard by which to assess peoples' choices. Not only did it universalize the value of enjoyment over pain (although some cultures may value pain), but it established a basic formulation that the "good" decisions were ones where total resulting pleasure outweighed total resulting pain. This lent itself smoothly to a more mathematical way of assessing ethics, a welcome change from a time when religious dogma had been the predominant measure. This approach has since become known as *cost–benefit analysis*; as already mentioned, it has risen to become a standard by which federal regulations are measured in Western countries born out of the utilitarian tradition. Seeing the world of regulation accordingly, economists began to think of legal rules as providing *incentives* or *disincentives* to behaviors considered socially useful or harmful (Wheelan 2010, 30). There are, of course, built-in assumptions here about what "society" is and does, but we will attend to those further along in this text.

Political-Economic

Closely related to the running ethical theme of utilitarianism are a series of political-economic ideas that are often viewed as essential to the application of the latter ethical framework. By political economy, I refer here to the ordering of power in society necessary for achieving prescribed economic ends, and the standards by which we are asked to measure whether those ends have been achieved. Themes therefore run the entire spectrum between politics and economics.

For example, *private property rights* is a subject that underpins much of the Law and Economics literature. In one important sense, these rights are indeed foundational to the legal order of the United States and other Western democracies. The founders of the American Revolution borrowed much of their philosophical platform from John Locke, who wrote that,

> Though the earth, and all inferior creatures, be common to all men, yet every man has a property in his own person: this no body has any right to but himself. The labour of his body, and the work of his hands, we may say, are properly his. Whatsoever then he removes out of the state that nature hath provided, and left it in, he hath mixed his labour with, and joined to it something that is his own, and thereby makes it his property. It being by him removed from the

> common state nature hath placed it in, it hath by this labour some-
> thing annexed to it, that excludes the common right of other men:
> for this labour being the unquestionable property of the labourer, no
> man but he can have a right to what that is once joined to, at least
> where there is enough, and as good, left in common for others.
>
> (Locke 1946)

Enshrining this into their formal Declaration of Independence, however, the founders changed this phrasing to "life, liberty, and the pursuit of happiness". Historians have speculated on the reasons for this—particularly since the founding class of revolutionaries tended to be propertied white men—but the most logical explanation is that the Declaration was intended to mobilize all colonial Americans to the independence movement, and it therefore needed to appear more inclusive. When the revolution was over and the war had been won, however, the phrasing used in the U.S. Constitution's Fifth Amendment returned to "life, liberty, and property". The understanding, going back to Locke, was that a key premise of central government in the new age of democracy was to be the State's role in securing individual ownership of private property. What could be privately owned, and to what degree, would remain a topic of debate ever since; but the understanding that government is primarily useful to protect property rights remains strong among many today, and notably among lawyer-economists.

Relatedly, *libertarianism* is a political-economic theme that permeates the history of Law and Economics. This philosophy holds that human liberty is paramount in matters of politics and economics, and that therefore decisions by the State, and arrangements in the economy, should be set up to foster the greatest degree of individual freedom. Not all lawyer-economists would call themselves libertarian. Nevertheless, the most high-profile among them have embraced this moniker, and several of the richest funding sources for Law and Economics research have been libertarian charitable foundations and non-university "think tanks" (Mayer 2016). Some of those organizations derive their endowments from family-run corporate organizations in industries such as petroleum, industrial chemicals, and ammunition—industries in which the federal government has strong interests, due to health, safety, and environmental protections, to regulate (2016). These foundations therefore have incentives in keeping the regulatory State *out* of the affairs of private business. This interest in small central government has been described as "anti-statism" by some (Teles 2018), but the term suggests greater uniformity and confrontation than is actually the case. Nevertheless, as one of the key themes in Law and Economics—which, recall, has tended to view market competition as superior to central planning of any kind—anti-statism may be a more accurate term for the political philosophy of most lawyer-economists than libertarianism would be today. That support for *market* forms of distribution is a third key political-economic theme to reflect upon. In the classic dichotomy, the two main alternatives in Western economic structures have been markets and command structures. Markets refers to a system in which individuals are free to set their own production levels, prices, and reinvestment goals; competition among separate firms or individuals becomes the only regulatory check on anti-social or self-interested behavior. A firm that sets its prices too high, or pollutes nearby lakes and rivers, will be disciplined in the marketplace—notably by consumer rejection. The trouble with this approach is that it demands that information be widely available and relatively "cost free". That would mean the costs of finding out regional prices, or of discovering which firms are polluting, are sustainable to everyone. In reality, this is rarely true. So, the self-interested activity competition intends to limit seems to flourish rather than dissipate in pure market systems.

Command structures are the opposite of markets. They refer to the type of economic system in which a government or other overseeing body (e.g., non-governmental organization, corporation) chooses critical features about the exchange system. Such features can include prices, quantities produced or sold, distribution channels, how profits are to be distributed (or not), and worker compensation. In the international arena, command structures have been associated most with communist and socialist systems originally intended to protect workers from the excesses of owners and employers. Since the end of the Cold War, even those systems have trended toward greater "liberalization" and slightly more relaxed command over some features of their economies. But by the same token, private corporations even in the West have sometimes been described as command structures: they, by definition, set the terms of exchange between members of the same firm, and members of their firm and outside agents. This comports with other accounts that view the group benefits offered to employees, as well as general employer–employee loyalty relationships, as inhabiting a form closer in shape to socialism than outright competitive capitalism. All of this leads to the observation that while corporate firms coexist and compete in highly competitive markets, they frequently are host to small internal command economies. Calabresi has called these "modified command structures" and he, following Ronald Coase (1937), Susan Rose-Ackerman (1985), and Katarina Pistor (2019), among others, believes these to have evolved among corporations as the more efficient model of organizational economy.

Similarly, Calabresi and Bobbit have explained that the very choice to put a price on some goods is a moral choice with sometimes unstated costs. They have labeled this "the cost of costing" (1978, 32). Most lawyer-economists do not attend to this feature of economic choices. To do so requires accepting that surrounding the economic behavior of individuals in markets is a layer of collective ethical decision-making about what items are "worth" putting a price on. An example of this unspoken dilemma can be seen in the market for human organs. In the United States, thanks to the 1984 National Organ Transplant Act, it is illegal to sell organs for money—hence there is no such market. But why? Surely there is high demand for life-saving organs such as kidneys, and each healthy person possesses two—one more than needed for survival. A classic Law and Economics approach might say that people should be free to sell their spare kidney for the right price, and that such capability would better allow organs to flow to those who would "value" them most.

This arrangement—and any law providing for it—would be more *efficient*, a key standard by which lawyer-economists assess good and bad law. Efficiency in this sense is not simply a matter of greater individual benefits than costs. It is an assessment that the benefits gleaned from a transaction make the distribution of greater benefits more desirable to the community in question. There are, to date, two main approaches to assessing efficiency in this way. The first is *Pareto efficiency*, after the Italian economist Vilfredo Pareto; in it, an economic arrangement is efficient if no other improvements can be made to that arrangement without costing some individual within it (Mornati 2013). The second approach is *Kaldor–Hicks efficiency*. Named for Nicholas Kaldor and John Hicks, this approach modifies Pareto efficiency to consider whether any new distribution would make everyone better *if* those who benefited from changes were made to compensate anyone harmed by such changes. This version of efficiency has proven especially popular in recent decades (Liscow 2018), and more will be said about it later in this book.

Psychological

By now it should already be clear that the simple assumptions about human behavior, ethics, and values that underpin Law and Economics are frequently themselves the subject of unspoken, or under-examined, "preferences" about the world held tacitly by experts performing these analyses. Only a few lawyer-economists have openly acknowledged this point (Calabresi 2016). But this is one of several key sites at which economic and sociocultural approaches to law can use one another's help to tell a more complete story of how law interacts with economic choices.

A second such place is in the domain of *rational choice* theory. It holds that individual human economic actors, left unencumbered by central controls, are rational value-maximizers—that they always act in their self-interest to maximize their benefits and minimize their costs. This idea sits at the heart of classical Western economics; it underpins other key ideas such as Adam Smith's "invisible hand" of the market, or Milton Friedman's conception of price as indicator of people's preferences. Economists have, for centuries, devised models for human behavior on the basic premise that people are rational actors, and this premise was imported wholesale into Law and Economics (Leitzel 2015, 58). Indeed, when the economics profession started to question this baseline assumption, it took lawyer-economists several years to catch up and to accept new models that account for people's *irrational* economic behavior. They were in part persuaded by the growing acceptance of *behavioral economics*, a new subfield rooted in psychology that studied people's conduct in real and simulated economic environments. The emerging lessons from economic psychologists such as Nobel laureates Dan Kahneman and Richard Thaler has been that human rationality is not uninfluenced by context and history, and we ought to consider this "bounded rationality". Several key lawyer-economists such as Katherine Zeiler (2016), Christine Jolls (2009) and Cass Sunstein (2000) have imported the lessons of behavioral psychology into their understandings of how law shapes economic preferences and choices. Sunstein and Thaler (2009) have stood out as offering some of the most concrete policy suggestions for U.S. lawmakers on the premise that a few relatively small legal innovations can "nudge" people's preferences away from unhealthy or unproductive choices—smoking cigarettes, for example— and toward more salubrious outcomes both individually (good health) and socially (lower shared costs of health care).

Sociological

It is not coincidental that lawyer-economists, faced with challenges to the presumption of human rationality, turned to psychologists first and foremost for guidance. Some have said that this reflects a shared view of the world that society is largely a collection of individuals. This allows psychologists to focus on individual behavior and to want to explain group dynamics in terms of individual actions. For lawyer-economists hoping to improve upon the rational actor without fully destabilizing the individualist long-embraced approach, behavioral psychology offered a relatively harmonious appendix to the existing theory.

The other important feature of lawyer-economist views about society arises in the familiar term *social welfare*. As stated above, welfarism has been at the heart of Law and Economics since the beginning—its roots lie in the utilitarian ethics that gave rise to economics as a discipline. Ordinary welfare refers to the goal of utilitarianism:

maximize well-being while minimizing harms to it. Social welfare emphasizes the aggregate well-being of the community; the "right" decision is that which increases welfare of the group on the whole. The important thing, however, is that the collective social welfare is not separate or above that of individuals, but rather the opposite: the well-being of a society is measured as the sum of well-being among its individual constituents (Ebenstein 2007). Once again, this assumes society is primarily a collection of individuals. Together, the embrace of behavioral psychology and the long-standing view of social welfare as aggregate individual welfare are two examples of the methodological individualism—and thus conception of society—Law and Economics is known for.

Legal

The final theme is itself legal in nature. It pertains to the proper role that law should occupy in a world where society is a collection of individuals, and where those individuals are presumed to be rational, or boundedly rational. In that world, the job of the law is to fairly and efficiently allocate costs imposed by one individual on another through physical injury, violation of a contract, or infringement on property rights through the pursuit of one's own self-interest.

Under the utilitarian ethical framework Law and Economics embraces, those kinds of costs are not necessarily unjustifiable. They can, instead, become highly justifiable depending on the benefits to be apparently gained. One could imagine a different framework leading to a different conclusion. Deontology is an alternative ethical approach that views duty (and its fulfillment) as the guiding force behind good decisions. In the example of organ trading, a deontologist might say we choose not to allow a kidney market because there is an inherent duty not to commoditize human flesh. Similarly, a deontologist might say one individual has a duty not to impose costs on one's neighbor just to pursue one's own profitable business or activity.

But the utilitarian framework says otherwise; one may impose costs on one's neighbor provided that they compensate or offset those costs in some fashion. Indeed, such costs ought to be considered in the initial cost–benefit analysis in the first place. This approach borrows from the economist Arthur Pigou who called these hidden costs to others *externalities*. A foundational belief in Law and Economics was that liability for these "negative" externalities should be imposed by the law to help achieve maximum economic efficiency; harm-creating actors will have to consider the costs imposed on others in deciding whether to pursue profits for themselves. The economist Ronald Coase later said this was wrong because both parties can value their benefits and costs themselves in deciding how to proceed (Coase 1960). If the victim were granted the right to freedom from a certain externality, the actor could "buy" that right from them for the victim's chosen price. If the actor were granted the right to produce the externality, the victim could "buy" that right for what the actor values it to be. Among the more libertarian lawyer-economists, the threat of coercion to extract compensation for externalities is the one true purpose of law (and the regulatory state) in society (Wheelan 2010, 56). For this reason, I have labeled this final theme a "legal" one. It reflects a certain conception about legal institutions and processes that is narrowly defined yet powerful in its capacity to set economic imbalances aright. And yet, if we accept that this should be the main purpose of law then we must consider other functions such as protecting basic rights to be secondary in nature.

Key Questions

From those themes, several major questions emerge and run throughout the rest of this book. These are questions that any new student or critic of Law and Economics should reflect upon as they venture through these ideas.

First, what is "society"? Obviously, the social sciences have long debated answers to this. Nearly all of them say that society is made from a web of relationships, and that these relationships are greater than the individuals connected by them. Most sociologists and anthropologists would say society is a unique phenomenon that arises when people *feel* themselves belonging to a large group;[3] sometimes they "find" themselves through the experience and other times they "lose" themselves. They see functional value in human society; an evolutionary advantage to it. This is very different from the way Law and Economics tended to view society as a collection of individuals, or transactions, or economic relationships primarily. Pushing back on this, one might ask if a society exists in situations of limited or no "exchange" of material goods. Would the lawyer-economists recognize that there may be important moments of exclusively "social" forms of being in society: meeting people, cracking jokes, talking about our families, and so forth—things that are economically non-productive yet socially generative? Whereas in the past they might not have, today many thoughtful lawyer-economists recognize the need for models of "society" that are more nuanced than the one previously embraced in the field. This probably will mean turning to neighboring disciplines such as sociology and anthropology more in the future (see Tejani forthcoming).

---

3 Durkheim called this feeling "collective effervescence" (2001).

Similarly, the preceding themes raise the question: what is "culture"? If economics refers to the system of production, distribution, consumption, and exchange, and if society is the distinct lifeworld created when individuals form large groups, that still leaves us wondering how to define culture. At face value most of us have some idea how this definition should look. Culture pertains to the symbols and images people develop to communicate; language is an easy illustration. But there's a lot more to consider: the everyday practices people engage in without thinking, the small rituals and ceremonies we perform around key life events (like blowing out candles on one's birthday), and so forth. Lastly and most importantly, there are *values* that comprise culture in ways no one can see, touch, or hear. Yet those invisible values are often the most significant cultural artifacts we have. As concerns Law and Economics, the question is whether any conception of "culture" has a role to play in economic analysis of law or legal analysis of economic policy. As this question will occur throughout this book, the short answer I wish to offer here is that culture should play a large role in these respects. Calabresi and Bobbitt (1978) acknowledge that difficult decisions we make when faced with scarce resources and high demand are often the product of culture. We, through our leaders, decide, for example, that a non-smoker is more deserving of a life-saving heart transplant than a smoker. This reflects a value judgment about which types of life are worth preserving, but it also creates a hierarchy of human lives—yet importantly, it is one most people can live with. Calabresi and Bobbitt explain that societies constantly struggle to arrive at such principles without destroying their self-conception as "social"—as caring for members and offering them fairness and compassion (1978, 18). But this observation can be taken further still. If culture helps to provide economic distribution with its moral license, then culture itself comes to have economic value—it becomes a "good" in itself as well (Calabresi 2016, 98).

The third remaining question is: what does it mean for people to be rational? It would seem that this has already been settled in Law and Economics. The first two waves of scholars simply assumed that, yes, people *are*—an assumption that transferred over from classical economics and Western legal philosophy. Without the basic premise of a fully formed rational actor, it would have been difficult to predict how people "tend to" behave when faced with material choices. Milton Friedman successfully pushed his discipline to become conspicuously predictive, so the rational actor became even more necessary in the late 20th century (Ebenstein 2007). But then came behavioral economics, inspired largely by research in psychology. Through experiments and empirical study, it showed that people do not uniformly follow "rational" models of behavior and choice. After some struggle, this was incorporated into mainstream economics, and then later into Law and Economics. So where has it left us today? With respect to human judgment, the most we can conclude is that sometimes people are rational, and other times they are not. Who or what now can teach us the *patterns* by which people switch between rational and irrational behavior? Are there social settings in which the community allows or even encourages one versus the other? These questions should linger for the remaining four chapters.

Next, a new reader of anything grounded in classical economics must ask: what is utility *really*? Contemporary economics embraces the ideas that individuals are "rational" in the sense of maximizing their own utility, and in the sense that the general welfare of society is a function of that society's utility (Wheelan 2010, 8–9). Here, "utility" differs from its customary lay meaning of "usefulness" or "helpfulness" and rather refers to all kinds of pleasure-generating qualities. So, a hammer has "utility" for the person who wishes to use it, but so does a ski resort under construction, or birthday cake, or a sports car. The latter three items are not typically tools used to create or fix other objects, but they are all items through which their consumer derives pleasure. They also come with "costs": a ski resort can destroy a mountain ecosystem, a cake may contribute to obesity, and a sports car can be driven recklessly to hurt a pedestrian. These negative externalities may not matter to the producer—who can profit from selling—or to the consumer—who benefits from using—but they do impact the community or society in which they occur. And to the economist studying these issues, they can matter a lot if that expert is concerned with general *welfare*. Welfare economists, which today are a substantial portion of the Law and Economics community, care about the distribution of goods and harms across the wider society. Thanks to their input, "utility" has come to be understood not as a merely individualized variable but also in terms of aggregate pleasure and pain—or "social utility", in the words of many. This aggregate definition of utility—given the importance of this term in general economic analysis—is a good thing, but it still contains some great limitations.

The single most important such limitation is about translation. If utility is about pleasure and pain, and social utility is about aggregating or "adding up" total pleasure and pain in a social system—for instance, the mountain area scheduled to be developed into a ski resort—the question becomes how to determine what we are adding up in the first place. This question, like so many underlying economic analyses, exceeds the scope of economic knowledge and expertise.

Last but not at all least, what is "freedom"? Most lawyer-economists do not speak explicitly about freedom, let alone define it. Yet the subject underlies so much about their work and their accompanying understandings of the world. The putative rational-actor subject of economic activity requires a basic level of human freedom. The strong faith in market exchange to achieve greatest efficiency through pricing rests upon a belief in human freedom. Even the so-called "irrelevance" of rights allocations argued by Coase is premised on a world of extreme human freedom (e.g., "zero transaction costs"). For these reasons, modern-day adherents of the classical economic theories—such as Adam Smith's "invisible hand" or his self-interested "baker"—find themselves closely allied with political theories that place human freedom ahead of other priorities. Libertarianism is one such political theory; many Law and Economics writers and research centers label themselves libertarian at the core.

This is not the place to raise original criticisms about this; however, it is important to note that placing freedom first can have deleterious effects on general welfare, and on distributive justice more specifically. In an economic system premised upon everyone unleashed to pursue *self*-interest, who is available and incentivized to look after the interests of the poor, the weak, or the otherwise vulnerable? What limitations would there be on individuals lobbying government for self-serving laws that benefit oneself by burdening others (e.g., regressive taxation). In a legal system premised on supporting the above economic system, how can law apply equally to the protection of everyone—including those with less economic agency? Is the solution to prioritize *social* well-being over individual freedom, or rather to strike some form of balance between these priorities?

Conclusion

This introductory chapter offered a panoramic picture of the terrain Law and Economics entered and shaped. It began with an overview of key legal subject areas where the subfield has held greatest influence: regulation, tax, business, criminal law, social welfare, and global finance and development. It then explored, in brief, "once-dominant themes" in the field. Among those ethical themes, it identified utilitarian and libertarian variants. The utilitarian strand included concepts of *utility*, *cost–benefit analysis*, *wealth-maximization*, and *efficiency*. Each follows an assumption that consequences matter most when evaluating a decision about law, policy, or society. Supplementing those, this section also described political, economic, material, psychological, social and legal themes running through Law and Economics simultaneously. These gave rise to several key questions left implied but unanswered in most of the literature. What is society? What is culture? Are people rational? What is utility? And finally, what is freedom? All pointed toward a strong demand for sociological or anthropological insights—ideas about things that cannot be separated from legal and economic behavior yet that Law and Economics alone does not explain or understand. Taking that perspective, one of the key conclusions is that Law and Economics—a field stereotypically fixated on individuals, on efficiency, and on small government—has been one of the most operative forces for *neoliberalism*, a political-economic worldview that views social welfare support as harmful to human freedom. Operationalizing this worldview has employed legal decisions, regulatory directives, and legislation—all items that Law and Economics has supplied and shaped. Lawyer-economists, therefore, have come to be viewed by some critics outside the subfield as technocrats responsible for operationalizing neoliberal ideas into policies that impact social life.

This seems like a damning conclusion, particularly if you care for the needs of others. Beyond the basic Western ethical philosophies of Utilitarianism, Kantianism, and Virtue Ethics, there emerged in the 1980s a new approach shaped by the social movements of the 1960s and 1970s—most notably feminism. In her 1981 book *In a Different Voice*, author Carol Gilligan described an "Ethic of Care"—an approach to right versus wrong that assesses decision-making based not on what benefits it brings in the end, nor what duty or obligation it complies with, nor the feeling of righteous personhood it procures, but rather based upon whether it reflects caring for the needs of others (Manning 2017). This Ethic of Care framework—now another tool for assessing ethical choices in the West—is most commonly raised by social science and humanities writers. It stands in stark contrast to the predominant consequentialist ethical posture of economics—and by extension of Law and Economics. The Ethic of Care, and the many who embrace it, stand opposed to the philosophies of neoliberalism, which they view as harmful to social cohesion and integration.

And yet, when a seemingly harmful idea holds popular support—particularly for this long—it is worthwhile to ask why. In this case, why might a worldview that priorities Self over Others, individuals over groups, and economic over social citizenship, be so successful in shaping governments and economies the world over? We are not the first to ask this. In the 1970s French theorist Michel Foucault, nearing the end of an influential career at the top of French intellectual life, came upon the ideas of neoliberalism and dedicated substantial attention to them in his 1978–1979 lectures at the Collège de France. Today, these lectures are read uncomfortably by social researchers. On one hand, Foucault presciently traces key features of the new neoliberal philosophy which would soon take hold among Western governments, namely in England and America, which systematically dismantled the social safety nets that helped usher them out of World War II. On the other hand, Foucault sees in this approach certain benefits to human freedom and autonomy.

Seemingly disillusioned by the French communists' and socialists' ability to promote human liberation, Foucault saw in the new neoliberal current, traces of hope. It offered a view of human autonomy rooted in individual choice rather than social control through bureaucratic coercion from inside or outside the State (Zamora and Behrent 2015).

As one might expect based on this introduction, Foucault's neoliberalism lectures are read dubiously today. Most curious to learn about them, or to use them in their own work, will likely be influenced by his earlier writings on asylums, prisons, sexuality—areas where deep history reveals the propensity for consolidation of power on the part of a centralized state. The earlier Foucault felt the solution was perhaps a decentralized state, or anarchism, in the political sense of the term. But his later work revealed that even non-state actors can serve the functions of governmental control, and that the panacea for human liberation might not result from *new forms* of governance but rather *less* of it entirely. The most telling aspect of this development for the purposes of this book, is that the mature Foucault favorably invokes the work of University of Chicago economist Gary Becker. Becker, who later won the Nobel Prize in economics, pioneered the idea of "human capital", published numerous works in prominent law journals, and became a collaborator with Richard Posner—the writer most associated around the world with Law and Economics (Becker and Posner 2009).

I wanted to conclude with this note on Foucault and neoliberalism as a reminder. Whatever it is we think we may know about ethics and freedom, and about Law and Economics' capacity or incapacity to advance those, it will be useful to remember that ideas are not simply interpretations of reality; they are subject to interpretations and reinflections in and of themselves. Law and Economics' stereotypical promotion of neoliberal thought, and the progressive Michel Foucault's constructive interest in the latter, are healthy reminders to suspend disbelief and to follow controversial ideas wherever they may lead, something the remainder of this book pursues vigorously.

References

American Bar Association, "2021 ABA Profile of the Legal Profession Highlights How the Pandemic Affected Lawyers." Americanbar.org, July 19, 2021. https://www.americanbar.org/news/abanews/aba-news-archives/2021/07/2021-aba-profile-of-the-legal-profession-highlights-how-the-pand/.

Baumgardner, Paul. 2019. "'Something He and His People Naturally Would Be Drawn To': The Reagan Administration and the Law-and-Economics Movement." *Presidential Studies Quarterly* 49: 959–975.

Becker, Gary, and Richard Posner. 2009. *Uncommon Sense: Economic Insights from Marriage to Terrorism.* Chicago, IL: University of Chicago Press.

Calabresi, Guido. 2016. *The Future of Law and Economics*. New Haven, CT: Yale University Press.

Calabresi, Guido, and Phillip Bobbitt. 1978. *Tragic Choices*. New York: W.W. Norton and Co.

Chotiner, Isaac. 2020. "The Contrarian Coronavirus Theory That Informed the Trump Administration." *The New Yorker*, March 29.

Coase, Ronald. 1960. "The Problem of Social Cost." *Journal of Law and Economics* 3 (Oct.): 1–44.

Coase, Ronald. 1937. "The Nature of the Firm." *Economica* 16 (4): 386–405.

Durkheim, Emile. 2001 [1912]. *The Elementary Forms of Religious Life*. Oxford: Oxford University Press.

Duxbury, Neil. 1995. *Patterns of American Jurisprudence*. Oxford: Clarendon Press.

Ebenstein, Lanny. 2007. *Milton Friedman: A Biography*. New York: St. Martin's Griffin.

Esptein, Richard. 2020. "Coronavirus Perspective: The Evidence Does Not Support Our Panicked Inferences." *Defining Ideas*, March 16, 2020. https://www.hoover.org/research/coronavirus-pandemic.

Ferri, Laurent. 2008. "Cornell and the Marshall Plan (1947–1951)." *Cornell International Affairs Review* 1 (2): 7–15.

Jolls, Christine. 2006. "Behavioral Law and Economics." Yale Law School, Public Law Working Paper No. 130, Yale Law & Economics Research Paper No. 342, Available at SSRN: https://ssrn.com/abstract=959177.

Kuhn, Thomas. 2012. *The Structure of Scientific Revolutions*. Chicago, IL: University of Chicago.

Leitzel, Jim. 2015. *Concepts in Law and Economics: A Guide for the Curious*. Oxford: Oxford University Press.

Leffler, M.P. 1988. "The United States and the Strategic Dimensions of the Marshall Plan." *Diplomatic History* 12 (3): 277–306.

Linebaugh, Peter, and Mark Rediker. 2000. *The Many-Headed Hydra: Sailors, Slaves, Commoners, and the Hidden History of the Revolutionary Atlantic*. Boston, MA: Beacon Press.

Liscow, Zachary. 2018. "Is Efficiency Biased?" *University of Chicago Law Review* 85: 1649–1718.

Liscow, Zachary. 2022. "Redistribution for Realists." *Iowa Law Review* 107:495–561.

Locke, John. 1946 [1689]. *The Second Treatise of Civil Government*, John W. Gough ed., Oxford: Basil Blackwell.

Manning, Rita. 2017. "Caring as an Ethical Perspective." In Fritz Allhoff, Alexander Sager, and Anand Vaidya eds. *Business in Ethical Focus: An Anthology*, 2nd ed. Petersborough, ON: Broadview Press, 56–61.

Mayer, Jane. 2016. *Dark Money: The Hidden History of the Billionaires Behind the Rise of the Radical Right*. New York: Penguin Random House.

Mornati, Fiorenzo. 2013. "Pareto Optimality." *Revue Europeene des Sciences Sociales* 51 (2): 65–82.

New York Times. 2022. "Coronavirus in the U.S.: Latest Map and Case Count." *The New York Times*. https://www.nytimes.com/interactive/2021/us/covid-cases.html. Accessed June 27, 2022.

Pistor, Katarina. 2019. *The Code of Capital: How Law Creates Wealth and Inequality*. Princeton, NJ: Princeton University.

Posner, Richard. 1981. *The Economics of Justice*. Cambridge, MA: Harvard University.

Rose-Ackerman, Susan. 1985. "Inalienability and the Theory of Property Rights." *Columbia Law Review* 85 (5): 931–969.

Sunstein, Cass, and Richard Thaler. 2009. *Nudge: Improving Decisions About Health, Wealth, and Happiness*, New York: Penguin Books.

Sunstein, Cass. 2000. *Behavioral Law and Economics*, Cambridge: Cambridge University Press.

Teles, Stephen M. 2008. *The Rise of the Conservative Legal Movement: The Battle for Control of the Law*. Princeton, NJ: Princeton University.

Wheelan, Charles. 2010. *Naked Economics: Undressing the Dismal Science*. New York: W.W. Norton.

Worldometer. 2022. https://www.worldometers.info/coronavirus/country/us/. Accessed June 27, 2022.

Zamora, Daniel, and Michael C. Behrent. 2015. *Foucault and Neoliberalism*. Cambridge: Polity.

Zeiler, Kathryn. 2016. "The Future of Empirical Legal Scholarship: Where Might We Go From Here?" *Journal of Legal Education* 66 (1): 78–99.

Chapter 1

Key Ideas

Introduction

The previous chapter offered a general picture of Law and Economics and some critical debates surrounding it today. This one presents the "key ideas" central to the movement in greater detail. These ideas have shaped legal doctrine and policy across virtually every area of Western law. This chapter explores this impact in three sections. The first, about "private law", refers to the legal rules and institutions that do not generally involve government (except at the stage of adjudication in courts). These will include the law of torts (accidents), contracts, property, and business. The next section will delve into two areas of "public law", which do directly implicate the government as a legal party: namely criminal and administrative law.

In many countries of the world, legal systems are divided organizationally and administratively into private law and public law. *Private law* refers to all legal rules and institutions applicable to disputes between individuals, between private organizations, or between an individual and an organization. This includes, for example, a contract dispute with a private employer, a nuisance claim between two residential neighbors, or a defamation suit by a celebrity against a tabloid newspaper. Private law therefore includes tort, contract, property, and business law most prominently among others. *Public law* refers to any legal rules or institutions applicable to disputes where the state, or the government, is a party. In most jurisdictions, the state is a party in criminal proceedings—hence the phrasing "People v. Jane Doe" or "State v. John Roe". Beyond criminal law, this can also include administrative law (e.g., agencies such as the Federal Trade Commission) and some aspects of constitutional law.

DOI: 10.4324/9781003350767-2

Private Law

Law and Economics has been very influential across all of these fields. In general, it has brought critical tools for assessing whether any particular rule or pattern in the law is the most productive for society. As described already, this usually comes down to an assessment of efficiency—even if that term is more complicated than generally stipulated. But despite the generality with which efficiency is used to assess legal doctrine and practices, there are some very specific ways in which its influence takes effect in the various subject areas of law. The next several sections unveil these in greater detail.

Tort Law

The law of torts, otherwise called "Tort Law" or simply "Torts", is a technical term for "a civil wrong not arising out of contract" (Abraham 2002, 1). As in all legal claims, a person harmed must assert that the wrongdoer owed them an initial *duty* not to commit the harm-creating act. This idea of duty has major ethical implications: we cannot say an action was "wrong" unless the actor was under some prior obligation not to engage in it. Indeed, it is that prior obligation which raises the specter that a wrong was committed according to some knowable principle. Without that, observers are simply applying some *ex post* judgment of the action based on a standard that the actor could never have known *ex ante*, and therefore could never have knowingly implemented. In order to declare something "wrong" in the Western world, we tend to prefer that there be a standard by which to measure this (e.g., a principle) and that this be known to the person responsible ahead of time.

What distinguishes the law of torts from the law of property and contract is the source for this known principle or obligation. Under property law, there are basic duties landowners assume *by virtue of their ownership of the property*. In some cases—as with covenants—these are written rules all neighbors cosign when purchasing a property. Under contract law, a similar observation can be made, except that the duty not to harm another person arises out of express or implied agreement. So, in the cases of both property and contract, the duty in question arises out of an existing legal relationship and memorialization of it: the deed or title on one hand and the written agreement on the other.

Under Tort Law there is usually no such prior relationship, and even more commonly no written agreement symbolizing it. There are only discrete encounters or acts between and among people. Taking for example a standard, run-of-the-mill car accident on the open highway, two drivers that collide traveling in opposite directions may have only seen each other briefly for a moment before impact, and before grave injury resulted. Perhaps the steering apparatus in one vehicle failed and caused it to swerve into oncoming traffic. Clearly, the rule cannot be that neither the driver—nor the manufacturer of the car, for that matter—remain "off the hook" because the victim was a perfect stranger; if so, then almost no accident would be legally compensated or discouraged. Instead, the practice for centuries in both common law and civil law countries has been to find a pre-existing duty *implicit in everyday social conduct*. In this case, it would read duty into the very fact that both drivers chose voluntarily to operate their motor vehicle on public roads that day. In other words, for Tort Law cases such as this, a duty arises from one driver to another by virtue of their mutual participation in risk-generating social behavior—namely driving from point A to point B. So the first key to understanding the law of torts is that its identification of duty is directly tied to its observance of social relationships.

But what does this duty consist of then? It is a duty not to drive perfectly but rather with "reasonable care". This is famously referred to as an "objective standard", as it considers optimal behavior to be something that results from ordinary good behavior rather than specific precautions or practices of any one particular safe driver. The so-called "objectivity" of this standard removes disagreements among individuals subject to personal tastes and finds rather a baseline of common behaviors most would consider "safe" under the circumstances.

This is precisely how legal *standards* are supposed to work. They are a type of precept similar to a "rule", but instead of articulating a clear behavior and a clear consequence for failing to conform to that, standards articulate a *range* of behavior that would be considered normal or lawful (Tejani 2019, 27). As lawyer-economist Louis Kaplow (1992) points out, rules can be more costly for lawmakers to develop whereas standards can be more costly for legal actors to interpret and follow. However, standards permit and respect a wider range of diversity of thought and action, and they offer legal decision-makers—judges and juries—spaces and times to consider the wisdom of community judgment. In other words, something like the reasonable care standard often becomes a matter of jury deliberation in close cases. What is meant by "close"? If a driver crashes into a pedestrian because their cell phone alarmed and distracted them with an emergency flash flood warning issued by the proper government authority, it may not be obvious that the driver behaved negligently, as this could potentially happen to anyone. A jury would be very helpful to consider this and issue a decision as to the factual question of whether distraction under these circumstances was unreasonable. But a driver who becomes similarly distracted while trying to purchase pre-sale tickets for a big pop concert would, in the mind of many judges, be considered more obviously "unreasonable" in their conduct. Such judges would likely not send the question to a jury, and the case would not be considered "close" on the issue of negligence. As you might already see, each situation brings with it a whole host of specific considerations, so creating a sharp, bright-line rule that it is always unreasonable to become distracted while driving may punish a lot of otherwise reasonable reactions to conditions in the real world. But let's just say the law of torts was overly strict in this way; then it might discourage or deter some behaviors that aren't actually wrong. What would be the problem with that?

Deterrence—discouraging wrongful conduct while leaving untouched useful or productive conduct—is, for some, one of the key functions of Tort Law, and something it shares in common with Criminal Law (Abraham 2002, 15–16). But creating deterrence too strictly runs the genuine risk of discouraging activities that create some good in the world. Driving is a good example: it carries major risks of personal and environmental harm, yet it is also the primary means by which people in many Western countries move about and participate in social and economic life. Discouraging bad driving alone is a good thing. Discouraging good driving, however, starts to negatively impact socio-economic participation. So where is the line between these?

Lawyer-economists have been working on this question for decades—it forms a key part of how they apply economic analysis to Tort Law. They call this pursuit of the right balance between overdeterrence and underdeterrence a search for "optimal deterrence". It signifies the level of behavioral encouragement and discouragement that most maximizes social and economic resources while best limiting conduct that would waste some of those resources. This search for a balance should sound familiar: it greatly resembles the pursuit of efficiency through the approaches mentioned in the last chapter. Much like the search for "Pareto Optimal" rules which would increase legal actors' wealth up to and until the level where it begins to decrease others', the search for "optimal deterrence" wants to limit risky conduct in society up to and until a level where doing so begins to reduce economic well-being. The word "optimal" in both phrases is doing the same work—it qualifies the goal as "maximum" efficiency.

When it comes to optimal deterrence and the reasonableness standard, one final important item to consider is whether and to what extent this approach allows for social change. Already, if we read Law and Economics from the perspective of sociology or anthropology, we must ask ourselves how much social and cultural practice and beliefs—and diversity within them—are respected and accounted for. But then, taking a historical perspective, we must also ask how the law under an economics framework—formalist by some descriptions—would allow for changes in social practice over time.

This led to the development of a second key "function" in the law of torts: loss distribution. Here, the question is not which precept allows for the most efficient behavioral controls, but rather what rule or decision about liability most efficiently distributes the costs of recovery between the parties, or across the community. An example arises from "mass torts" such as bridge and tunnel disasters, gas leaks, and oil spills. In the event of one of these accidents, a large company is often responsible for negligently operating or maintaining the infrastructure or equipment; frequently, though not always, this negligence is the result of attempting to save ahead of time on safety costs. In the era of "shareholder value" primacy—described elsewhere in this book, such short-term cost-saving decisions and the accidents they can lead to seem to have grown more palatable. This may be because more and more regular citizens have become investors or shareholders through pension systems and retirement investing. But along with the companies that attempt to save shareholder resources, there are also often thousands of victims who suffer economic harm when these accidents take place. Limiting the *scope of liability*, as this is often called, is an approach to loss distribution that emerged from the economic analysis of torts to avoid exorbitant costs being passed to private companies in such situations.

Finally, the last major way in which lawyer-economists shaped this area of the law was with the realization that torts and property law are best imagined on a continuum depending on social circumstances. In 1972 Calabresi and Melamed published "Property Rules, Liability Rules, and Inalienability". The article argued that the seemingly separate areas such as property and torts are actually two *connected* approaches to rights allocation. Whereas common law had evolved to view these as separate, progressive solutions to contemporary legal problems such as environmental pollution might entail departing from the "natural" application of these approaches. Indeed, greater flexibility in using these approaches would better account for inequality and the way it changes experiences of the law and legality. So, for example, in the case of an air pollution nuisance case, a homeowner may wish to stop a horse stable from operating next door due to noxious smells and waste products that pose an environmental health risk to the homeowner. A *property* rule might recognize the homeowner's latent right to an environmentally safe use of her property, and it would enjoin (e.g., immediately stop) the horse stable from operating. Or it might recognize the polluter's inherent right to use its land for horses and allow it to continue without any penalty. A *liability* rule, meanwhile, might declare the stable to be a "nuisance" but would allow it to continue if it paid sufficient damages (e.g., money) to the neighboring resident. Or it might reverse this liability so that the stable could operate unless and until the neighbor pays to enjoin its actions. Each rule creates a slightly different dynamic as to the relationship between the parties, but each could be valid from the standpoint of rights. Moreover, the choice between these different rules and initial entitlement—with the stable or the homeowner—can and often does make a difference from the standpoint of "efficiency". One might lead to the most valuable use of the two properties, whereas the others may not.

Contracts

Given its importance to commerce and market transactions, it is no surprise that contract law has been subject to considerable influence from Law and Economics. Whether and how to interpret contractual agreements may be significant to any particular transaction or dispute, but it can also have widespread implications for "efficiency" if indeed that is an overarching policy goal to be served—complications about the term and its presuppositions notwithstanding. As already described, the origin of "duty" in contract law lies in bilateral agreements themselves. And yet, as Law and Economics has influenced this field, it has seemingly drifted toward recognizing more reasons for avoidance—as always to serve efficiency goals. Two key doctrines illustrate this drift.

The first is "at will employment". Far from a new innovation of the late 20th century, the at-will doctrine has origins in the common law dating to the 19th century. Prior to that, as articulated by English jurist William Blackstone, the default rule said that all employment agreements would be interpreted to last a fixed term unless otherwise modified contractually (Blackstone 1755). This was the default English common law principle. So, it is noteworthy that in 1877 American jurist H.G. Wood, in a treatise about master–servant law, articulated an opposite rule based on a line of four cases in the American courts (Biasi and Tuzet 2016). The presumption in cases where no term of employment was specified, Wood stated, was that the relationship could be terminated by either employer or employee *at any time* without notice and without just cause. As Biasi and Tuzet (2016) point out, it was remarkable that Wood had effectively "invented" a rule that was then quickly accepted as customary, despite centuries of precedent to the contrary. The move bears striking resemblance to what historians, following Eric Hobsbawm, have come to call "invented tradition": the adoption of a new holiday, practice, ceremony, or symbol as though it had always, already existed (see e.g., Tejani 2019).

But the most interesting aspects of the at-will employment doctrine for our purposes is not where it comes from (and doesn't) but how it has been justified over time. When an employer can dismiss an employee without notice or cause, several things result. For instance, the employee must live with a certain degree of insecurity. Whereas under the previous system workers could not be let go simply because the company feared financial hardship, today they can be.

At-Will Employment Policies by State

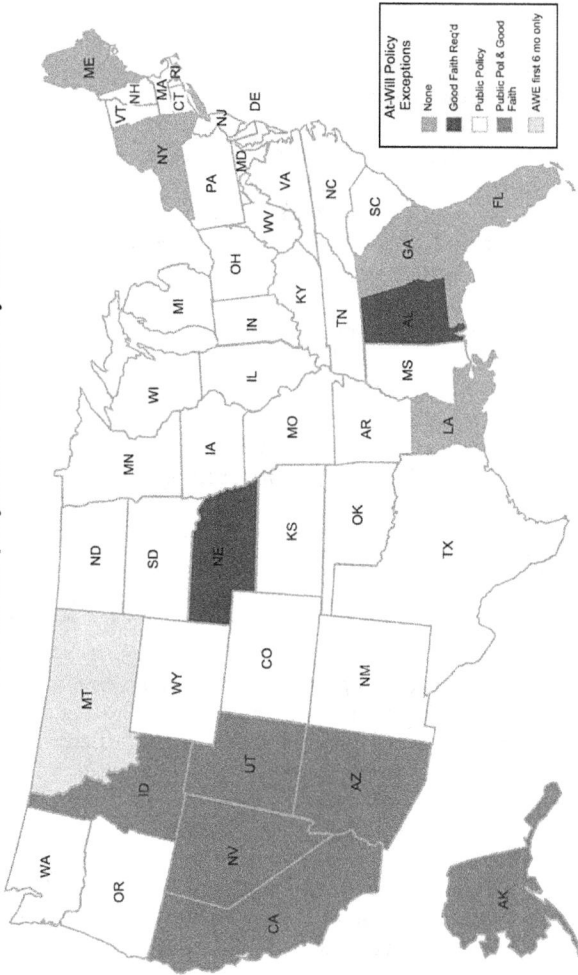

At-Will Policy Exceptions
- None
- Good Faith Req'd
- Public Policy
- Public Pol & Good Faith
- AWE first 6 mo only

Figure 1.1 U.S. states with "at-will employment" laws and public policy exceptions. Every state except Montana permits full at-will employment after the first six months of employee hiring.

This means that sudden shifts in market demand for certain products, or in the costs of raw materials such as timber or crude oil, can have a direct and immediate impact on workers. This, in effect, makes their labor a bit more like a natural resource and a bit less, therefore, like a human one. Or perhaps similarly, it reduces human resources to simply "labor". The final and perhaps most significant toll taken by the at-will doctrine is that it diminishes feelings of "due process". Due process is the constitutionally enshrined guarantee that a person should receive a hearing before basic rights or entitlements are taken from them. We think of this most often in the criminal law context, where incarceration—loss of freedom—is a common consequence for a finding of "guilt". In the employment context, some have said, the right to work approaches a similar level of importance because of how connected this is to other basic needs such as food, water, and shelter. Under at-will employment, a worker can be dismissed without any hearing about their conduct or position. This appears to violate due process in both the *procedural* sense—that a formal process should be followed—and in the *substantive* sense—that the merits of the dispute should be adequately weighed. So, if this many ills result from the at-will doctrine, then why keep it? This is where it gets interesting.

Richard Epstein, the lawyer-economist cited early in the last chapter, spelled out the following strengths about the system (1984). First, it embraces "freedom of contract", which neo-classical market economics and political liberalism are based upon. If contracts can be defeated without expensive showings of "cause", then parties are freer to enter into them because the stakes are lower. Furthermore, parties are free to terminate them immediately upon experiencing dissatisfaction, thereby freeing themselves to enter a new agreement with a new opposing party. Secondly, they point to the "freedom of movement" benefit of at-will employment. If a worker feels he or she might be valued more in another firm, they are free to move on; *or*, if an employer feels it can get better value from recruiting a new laborer, they are free to move on—or more precisely move the newcomer *in*. These possibilities support the free movement of labor that many feel is an important facet of free-market economies. Assuming that labor *could be* treated like other resources, its freedom of movement would be a key premise behind any hope that it will flow to the employer who assigns it the highest value. And finally, writers point out that at-will agreements promote greater efficiency. Employees, unprotected by a formal contract term, will be retained based on their ongoing performance, thereby incentivizing their highest quality and quantity of work, and thereby maximizing value for the employer and its investors. Similarly, employers, also unprotected from sudden labor stoppages, are incentivized to value workers at the highest possible level to avoid employee departures or, worse, reputational damage that might deter prospective employees.

If at-will employment says it is acceptable to quit or be fired on one's first day or first week on the job, could it be similarly acceptable to avoid *any* contract upon discovering a better deal somewhere else? Any answer to this question must first unravel what, exactly, a contract even is. Formally speaking, a contract is an *enforceable promise* commemorated by an *offer*, an *acceptance*, and *consideration*—a legal term meaning something exchanged with at least some value. Together these elements speak to the issue of contract formation. Once they are all present, we say that a contract has been formed, and the parties are now obligated to "perform". Performance then comes down to whatever is specified in the agreement; for some it will mean paying sums of money at stated intervals; for others it will mean rendering important services such as painting a house, performing surgery, or writing a book. And here is where it gets tricky, because sometimes—after the terms of the agreement have been established and agreed to—conditions change, or new information comes to light—and it becomes *more expensive* to "perform" than to not. The costs of paint might have tripled, or the insurance industry may have changed reimbursement rates for a particular operation. Furthermore, these added costs may start to exceed the likely damages one would have to pay from violating a formal contract. In these cases, one of the parties may decide it is cheaper to walk away and pay the penalty than to fulfill an "enforceable promise" he or she undertook to complete (Leitzel 2015, 42).

In the Law and Economics of contract law, this is called "efficient breach". It means that, while indeed a promise was broken, and while the violating party may have to pay liquidated damages (e.g., a penalty for walking away), a court will recognize that this is an economically necessary choice and allow the violating party to pay damages and move on. It will therefore preclude the other side from the equitable remedy of "specific performance"—in other words it will not compel the parties to perform.

This relatively new development in contract law has been supported by well-known lawyer-economists for some time (see Leitzel 2015). But notice what it does to our basic understanding of a contract. If we are told that the foundation of contract is an "enforceable promise", and that the origins of duty in contract come from this promise, then the duty to fulfill ones obligation comes from a source located in the moral relationships the parties have established with one another. It does not, in other words, come from any actual or "real" assessments of the consequences of the agreement. Indeed, some might say the entire purpose of a contract is to protect the parties from any changes in those consequences—things such as changes in the price of paint or insurance reimbursement rates. In the language of moral philosophy, this notion of contractual responsibility is *deontological*—it stems from the voluntary assumption of a duty in itself.

Efficient breach suggests the opposite. It implies that the origins of contractual duty are tied to the projected consequences of the agreement—for instance, expected profits—and that changes to those consequences can alter the enforceability of that duty at any time. This appears to remove the *a priori* protection that contract affords in a shifting market economy. And yet, lawyer-economists would likely respond that the material outcome—whether the aggrieved party receives the goods and services, or whether it receives a cash substitute—is economically the same. It is, they would say moreover, more efficient to allow this because it maximizes resources allowing the violator to sell his or her goods and services to a higher bidder, while forcing them to render the victim of the breach "whole" as though the contract had been performed.

All this highlights apparently diverging conceptions of duty in contract situations. Many economists would likely see the "promise" of the initial contract as contingent on market conditions. But many sociologists and anthropologists, not to mention philosophers, would see the promise as, in fact, the basis for an entire web of social relationships necessary to the formation of a market in the first place. In other words, the social connections implied and preserved by promises—be they personal or collective, gratuitous or commercial—may have significance far beyond the economic sphere and shape social cohesion itself. It is a debate that becomes difficult to resolve across the theoretical and methodological divides separating economics from other social sciences, and yet it lies at the heart of the controversies over neoliberalism covered elsewhere in this book.

Property

The duties one owes to people as a result of ownership or possession of land have their origin in their rights of control. If you are the owner, for example, of a vacant lot (e.g., an empty plot at the back of a neighborhood), you have a series of rights stemming from your claim of control that includes *inter alia* the right to exclude others from your property. However, if your property contains an object that might be of special interest to the neighborhood children—an old rusty trampoline, for example—and if that object is so old or neglected that it poses a danger to the kids, then this can be classified an "attractive nuisance" and you will be held liable for any injury visited upon a child who ventures onto the property to play with the trampoline. This is true despite the fact that the kids would be on the parcel of land as "trespassers". Attractive nuisance is but one example of many in which a landowner incurs duties—sometimes to perfect strangers—simply by holding ownership control.

This phenomenon is related to a more general conception in property law that has resulted from economic influence. It holds that a person does not actually "own" a parcel of land or a piece of personal property (for example, a laptop computer) but rather they own a "bundle of rights" associated with that property. That bundle would normally include things like *the right to exclude others* as seen above, *the right to use, the right to improve, the right to alienate or transfer*, or *the right to subdivide* the property. The right to exclude others is self-explanatory, on the face of it, but its implications are more complex. While it could mean that you are justified in escorting trespassers off your land at various moments throughout the day, it more likely means in practice that you have the right to build a fence or wall around the property. It also helps to ensure minimal interference with some of the other rights listed. It guarantees, in other words, *exclusivity* of ownership. This is significant in broader perspective, because the right to *private* ownership distinguishes Western legal cultures from non-Western and indigenous ones that recognize collective or family ownership only, but that might ensure wider distribution of benefits resulting from exploitation of the land and its resources. This relates, in turn, to the right to use the property. It entails a right to extract resources from the land, or to employ a personal item like a computer, even when that use may itself devalue the land or object in question. It is similar to the right to exclude in the sense that both are about isolating the land or object from others: exclusivity separates the piece from others spatially; use separates the piece from others temporally—it discounts claims of *future* or *past* owners who may care whether the remaining trees are cut down or the stream is polluted. Somewhat opposingly, the right to improve a property or object is another key aspect of ownership recognized in this "bundle of rights" identified by lawyer-economists. It holds that the claimant has the right to build on, renovate, modify, or otherwise transform the property in ways that *increase* its value. But more to the point, it also means the holder carries the right to benefit from that increased valuation as well. This leads in turn to the right of alienation—the entitlement to sell or trade the property at the holder's discretion, and therefore discretionary price. One can imagine very well a system in which any sale of a property must be channeled through the state or other central authority. The reasons for such oversight might include distributive fairness—making sure everyone has access to ownership and the resulting rights it entails. But Western legal systems generally don't embrace this kind of central oversight of property transactions; on the contrary, they foster the kind of free-market transactions that maximize sale or rental prices, and they provide the "recording" systems to ensure official transfers (of real property that is) are duly memorialized and unfalsifiable. And lastly, one of the key rights held within the "bundle" recognized by economists of property law is the right to subdivide a parcel or property. In some instances, subdivision might destroy or devalue a property, such as with a public greenspace or park; in other cases, it only increases the overall value. In most cases, the owner will only engage in this if it benefits them to do so. And yet, we leave this to owners—though permits may be required in some cases—as part of their integral set of rights of ownership, rather than maintaining central authority over property sizes.

This "bundle of rights" approach was developed by the "Property Rights" school of neo-institutionalist Law and Economics developed in the 1960s by scholars such as Gary Becker, Harold Demsetz, and Steven Cheung (Mercuro and Medema 1997, 132). Neo-institutionalism focused mostly upon the rules and procedures that make law so important to economic exchange, wealth creation, and distribution. They are, as some say, the "rules of the game" that people such as Milton Friedman allude to as the *only* proper constraints on free-market activity and firms that constitute it. This perspective on property represented a departure from conventional wisdom which saw *value* emerging from the possessed object itself. After the neo-institutionalists,

> [W]e recognize ... that individuals derive utility, not from goods and services per se, but from the various attributes of a good or the various separate activities that go into the performance of the service. That a plot of land is not just a plot of land per se, but a bundle of attributes including the extent of his agricultural productivity, aesthetic qualities, or potential for commercial development of various kinds. ... The result is that exchanges not merely the transference of goods and services, but of bundles of diverse attributes and activities.
> (1997, 134)

On one hand, this approach appears congruent with some social science perspectives on property. Marcel Mauss, ethnologist and disciple of French sociologist Emile Durkheim, famously wrote—about non-Western gift economies in the Pacific Northwest and in the South Pacific—that many objects are valuable not in their potential "use" but in the social relationships they represent. Thus, conspicuous and lavish gift-giving can run counter to a giver's purely economic self-interest but can consolidate his (usually a male Chief) or her social power in a community (Mauss 2000). Similarly, it can help to consolidate power across tribes. Most dramatically, Mauss writes, the unreciprocated gift can leave the recipient incomplete, as it transfers a part of his or her *hau* or spirit to the giver (2000). The property given, in other words, is less about the material object than about the attributes and activities it comes to represent and accrues over time.

On the other hand, the bundle-of-rights approach seems in harmony with Western ideals about property ownership and the connections many believe it has to human freedom. It was Locke, political theorist and inspiration for certain key Western legal institutions, who argued that one of the main purposes of "political society" was to collectively protect individual private property interests (Locke 1946). This was because, if individuals and families were left alone to produce and consume their own goods, some would inevitably innovate labor-saving, or efficiency-boosting techniques that would increase their own production, raise their land value, and result in surpluses that could be traded for more goods (1946). Freedom to produce, in other words, would lead to naturally resulting inequalities. Protection of one's surplus wealth or value, in turn, would help to protect individual investments of extra time and labor, and it would in turn incentivize innovators to continually produce more. Private property rights guaranteed by a central state authority, in other words, were one of the main drivers of economic development and growth and one of the greatest premises for state power. As in the Maussian explanation for property attributes above, the land and goods it yields are not valuable only in themselves but in the capacities and opportunities they afford their possessors. But unlike for Mauss, whose primary purpose is to explain widescale exchange of objects with almost no "use value", Locke's private property (and view of human freedom) helps to explain why and how we *do not* exchange valued goods, and rather how, with state sanction, we are licensed to hold them—sometimes even to the detriment of our neighbors.

One of the most significant innovations in the economics of property disputes makes use of this connection between property and freedom. In 1960, the British economist Ronald Coase argued that the allocation of property rights such as the kind described above—in other words, the choice to assign such rights to one party or another in a property dispute—is relevant *only* because the costs for the parties to come to their own agreement are prohibitively high (1960). It suggested both that transaction costs should be minimized to try to permit freer bargaining between the parties and that law's only objective if it intervenes at all should be to simulate such a free bargain by, in other words, assigning rights to the most efficient user of them (1960).

Coase himself was part of the neo-institutional school of economics which believed that economics should be understood with respect to the rules and processes that set up markets or command structures (Mercuro and Medema 1997). His 1937 article "The Nature of the Firm" introduced "transaction costs"—which became the focus of neo-institutionalists for decades after (1997). There, he suggested the whole purpose of firms in market economy was to reduce the costs of transactions that commercial actors would otherwise incur.

In 1960, he wrote that transaction costs were the only reason why law needed to get involved in disputes over property use. The archetypal case would be a nuisance dispute much like the one discussed above. One property owner wants to operate a horse stable that produces manure and noxious smells as a byproduct of equestrian activities for commercial gain. The neighboring owner wants a clean and quiet rural environment to raise children and host weekend barbeques. If the neighbor sues the stable, who should win? Coase's 1960 article said "it doesn't matter" because in a free-market environment the party who places the greatest value on their own use (recreational or residential) will have the incentive to "buy out" their rival. That said, courts should attempt to assign the use right to the party with the most "valued" use (1960).

For the 1937 and 1960 articles, Coase was later awarded the 1991 Nobel Prize in economics. In 1964 he was also appointed editor of the *Journal of Law and Economics* after being recruited from the University of Virginia to replace Aaron Director at the University of Chicago Law School. Coase was, in other words, considered to be a jewel in the crown of the Chicago School. And yet, he was far from its greatest cheerleader. In the 1950s he declined an offer to join the university (Medema 2021). He favored qualitative research methods over regression analysis preferred by his contemporaries (2021). And most importantly, he felt that his initial paper on transaction costs had been taken too far out of context by lawyer-economists in the decades of rapid growth within Law and Economics (Schwartz 2013). "Absent transaction costs" became a popular refrain among writers in the latter 20th century, and yet Coase himself said that such a world was implausible (Frank 2013). Indeed, with his neo-institutionalist orientation, he was against such counterfactual studies and predictions of economic behavior—though this hesitation has been generally forgotten. And yet, the ambivalence he felt toward subsequent uses of those tools would foreshadow several of the challenges many—sociologists and anthropologists of law especially—would direct at the field in the ensuing years.

Business Law

The influences of Law and Economics on business law have been at once more diffuse and pronounced. Several of the main research centers for Law and Economics in the United States have adopted missions and titles incorporating "business".[1] This is based on a seemingly "natural"

---

1 See e.g., Stanford, Texas, Northwestern.

fit between the fields, and yet realization of such overlap was not natural at all—it came from deliberate efforts on the part of institution builders and intellectual entrepreneurs.

From the beginning, two of the institutional founders of the movement envisioned and promoted its influence in the business sector. Aaron Director, at the invitation of Frederick von Hayek, was present for the Mont Pelerin Society meetings in Switzerland circa 1947—which many feel inaugurated the Chicago School. There, Director's comments, "warn[ed] that the 'collectivist' claim that the greater efficiency of large-scale business enterprises made private monopolies inevitable" (Kolasky 2020). Director's solution to the regrettable overlap between firms and command economies, in turn, was to develop a "legal framework in order to design a more effective 'competitive order' and thereby reduce the need for government regulation" (2020). For Director, therefore, one of the foundational purposes of Law and Economics was to set up guardrails for competition in American business that would obviate the need for government regulation.

This objective would come even more into focus in the work of Henry Manne. Known today alongside Director as one of the two great institutional entrepreneurs for Law and Economics, Manne would be the first outside Chicago to build and propagate centers for Law and Economics research, first at Emory, then at Miami, and finally at George Mason where he was founding Dean, and where the center he created carries his name and remains most active today. Before all this, Manne was a corporate law specialist who wrote favorably about the disciplinary effect of "hostile takeovers" and the informational effects of "insider trading" (Teles 2008, 102). Moving from his own research into institutional governance and development, Manne argued that the economic approach to law would be fundamental to the shape of business law in the 20th century. What he envisioned was a new facet of legal education in America: "The idea should be to infuse the entire curriculum with economic sophistication. Law graduates who plan on careers in government, in business or with business law firms should be equipped to analyze the problems they confront with rigorous analytic techniques of both law and economics" (quoted in Teles 2008, 103).

It wasn't simply that modern legal education infused with the new economic tools imported into law in Chicago *could* be of use to commercial industry; it was, for Manne, that partnerships between American business firms and law schools should be a logical step. As he put it,

Almost every corporation today has considerable in-house legal work; the general counsel has become an increasingly important figure; and the promotion of general counsels into higher executive offices is quite common in American industry. Thus a law school especially designed to serve the needs with which these men are familiar could strike a responsive chord that many other law schools do not.

(quoted in Teles 2008, 103)

Thus, a business-oriented law school founded on economic theoretical assumptions and methods became a dream of Manne from his early days at the University of Rochester. There, while on faculty in the department of political science, he proposed to create such a law school for the University on the belief that financial resources for the institution could come from private industry itself. Moreover, Manne wanted the school to differ from virtually all others in the country at the time by emphasizing an underlying *libertarian* posture (Teles 2008, 104). This turned out to be the project's albatross: he could not sell many wealthy donors, some university faculty, and the local bar on his idea (2008, 104). So, the Rochester School of Law grounded in economic analysis of law became a dead letter, and Manne focused his efforts instead on the pedagogical project of educating U.S. law professors in economic theory and methods directly—an effort that would prove to be enduringly influential and consequential in American legal academia.

Moving from the founding purposes of Director and Manne, the substantive contributions of Law and Economics revolutionized business law in a few key ways. Minimal government constraints along with minimal ancillary activities among corporate firms—Hayek and Friedman felt—were key to establishing the most accurate pricing of goods and services in the hopes of achieving the most efficient balance between supply and demand in the economy. This meant that corporate projects outside the usual production, distribution, marketing and sales, were a kind of noise in the economic system. Friedman would write that the only true social responsibility of business is to make as much profit as possible (1970). Against the pressures of the environmental, civil rights, and women's movements of the era, Friedman believed that companies engaging in social causes were effectively stealing money from the pockets of investors—particularly offsite public shareholders, who he and others have argued are the true owners of companies (1970).

Within just a few years of Friedman's famous essay on social responsibility, Richard Posner would come to make a parallel argument about the law. Justice, an ephemeral concept whose definitions vary between communities and cultures, should actually be measured by aggregate *wealth maximization* defined first by Pareto optimality and later by Kaldor–Hicks efficiency (1973). This development is treated at greater length elsewhere in this book, but here I use it to suggest a unique harmonization that took place in the period from the 1950s to the 1970s between Director, Manne, Friedman and Posner: through them, and through the theories afforded by Law and Economics—particularly the Chicago variant, the relationship between law and business was forged ever stronger by an alignment of *ethical* purposes.

The preceding section has examined the influence of lawyer-economists in the areas of tort, contract, property, and business law. Each of these belongs to the domain frequently called "private law" for its regulation of conduct and disputes between individuals, among private organizations, or both. The common denominator of these is the absence of government or state involvement except at the stage of adjudication—in other words of "court". The next section shifts to discuss just two areas in what is called "public law", the arenas in which the state does in fact play a role as one party.

Public Law

The private law and public law distinction is more pronounced in legal systems outside of England and the United States. France's legal education system, for example, divides these two areas into *droit privé* and *droit publique* with disputes in either being sent to a distinct court system with separate courts of appeal and last resort. But even though the United States does not observe this distinction so formally, it does separate its legal subject matter similarly and approaches the application of law in "public" disputes matters uniquely. Economic theory and analysis have shaped these areas differently as well.

Criminal Law

Criminal law is the first clear example of an area where one party to any disputes is always the State. While we may not have two fully separate court pyramids for them, the English and American legal systems do distinguish between civil and criminal law cases in part by sending them to different courts of first instance—or trial courts. Hence, the Superior Courts of the State of California distinguish between Civil Division (for personal injury claims) and Criminal Division (for crimes). From a Law and Economics perspective, there are a few different reasons for treating criminal law differently.

The first has to do with the economic role of crime itself. There are various reasons why some activity might be declared by the community or the society as a "crime". One could be that the activity results from or promotes a version of morality that the community or society does not—as a whole—share. So, for example, polygamy, the marriage of one person to two more other people, has been a federal crime in the United States since 1882. There is not an immediate economic reason for why this should be the case, but it does seem to enforce a fundamental Judeo-Christian moral belief that marriage is a "union between one man and one woman". Then again, there may be unstated but still important economic dimensions to the practice of polygamy; if one man can marry multiple wives, this could indirectly impact the ability for other men to find partners, marry, reproduce, and generate human resources for the next generation to carry on the community. Or, as a sociologist or anthropologist might remind us, these economic implications are speculative without more direct evidence. In any case, there are certainly other more obvious crimes in which economics are at play. Property crimes such as theft, burglary, embezzlement, and so forth may be considered morally "wrong", but they are treated with different punishments for specific reasons; witness, for example, the treatment of "white-collar" crimes such as embezzlement in comparison to theft and burglary when even the dollar amounts in question might be vastly larger in the case of the former. Here, many would argue that while both are property crimes, the former involves little chance for violence and physical harm whereas the latter do increase the possibility of these. Regardless of all these nuances, there is some consensus that the types of activities determined to be "criminal" in the Western world are frequently ones whose economic benefits do not outweigh their moral damage to the community, or ones with no economic benefit to the community at all.

For this reason, the penalty for activities deemed a "crime" is usually *punishment*. If that seems obvious and self-explanatory, consider for a moment that punishment or punitive justice is only one form alongside other possibilities. Outside the criminal system, punishment is rarely applied, even after a finding of liability by a judge or jury. Instead, the civil system tends to apply compensatory justice in the form of monetary damages for victims of both intentional and unintentional wrongs. In some cases, restorative justice is applied through "equitable" remedies intended to restore the victim to its original position prior to wrongdoing. So, for example, the equitable remedy of "specific performance" would require a contract violator to perform on the promises made as part of the contract agreement even though the violator prefers not to, and even though monetary damages could otherwise be applied. Specific performance and other equitable relief are used especially in cases when money would be insufficient to make the victim whole. In any event, whether compensatory or restorative forms of justice apply, or whether money damages or equitable relief are required, these forms of civil remedy are different fundamentally from punitive justice which seeks to exact a penalty from the wrongdoer. In the criminal justice system, that penalty is often taken as monetary fines, but it is also frequently in the form of the defendant's own freedom—that is to say, incarceration.

The classification of activities subject to punishment and the magnitude of these punishments are usually decided by legislatures. Criminal codes are drafted, ratified, and amended by legislatures at either state or federal level. This means that the written rules about crime must be specific enough for judges to understand what the legislature intended, but general enough to accommodate new evolutions in criminal conduct. For example, does digital misappropriation of cryptocurrency or NFTs from someone else's computer or device without their consent constitute the crime of "theft", or must it go unprosecuted until lawmakers get around to writing it into the criminal code? In any event, the lesson is that for criminal law in our modern era, the rules are written and compiled by professional lawmakers in highly organized codes, which in turn are meant to be accessible and understandable to everyone. But it is noteworthy that some activities—drug use, for example—catch the eye of legislatures quickly and starkly whereas others—for instance cryptocurrency fraud—only do so *after* significant harms have been allowed. How do societies decide what should be unlawful as a crime and what should not, or when the decision about this can or should be reached only later?

In Law and Economics, the study of how societies decide such things through legislatures is known as *public choice* theory. Public choice sits at the apex of law, political science, economics, and sociology. It asks how the law and policymaking process can be viewed and studied as adjunct to economic market behavior itself. For instance, if a society is faced with the extinction of an owl species from a forested part of its territory, it might wish to protect that species by limiting timber harvesting (e.g., tree cutting) in the region for a set period of years. Doing this might save the owls from extinction, but it would almost certainly decimate the local logging industry and cost thousands of jobs—that is to say people's livelihoods. Suppose the lawmaking body of that region, faced with debating and adopting the law, votes narrowly against it. A simple explanation might conclude that the "will of the people" was to save the logging jobs, not the owls, and walk away. But a more nuanced public choice study of this case might find that the logging industry had millions of dollars to spend convincing lawmakers that the new rule was bad for everyone. It might have even spent some of that money urging citizens to pressure their representatives to see it that way. The environmental groups, however, might have had no such lobbying treasure chest to spend from, but they might have had several noteworthy celebrities to make public announcements and appearances to convince the same stakeholders. In that case, the battle could be framed as one between two competing economic interests and their separate partisans. In any case, it should be clear that the decisions lawmakers come to in developing new rules—for instance what constitutes a new "crime"— are far from merely an expression of the "will of the people".

To understand what is at stake behind Public Choice theory, it is useful to consider the economic functions of criminal law. We have already stipulated that activities deemed "criminal" tend to have a lesser economic value to the community than those deemed unlawful in other respects, for example under tort or contract law. But even though it may not directly regulate economically "useful" activity, the criminal law itself can be said to serve important economic functions by, in effect, establishing and enforcing the boundaries of legitimate economic activity. Three such boundaries merit special attention. The first is to reduce "negative externalities". This term can be taken to mean any harmful byproduct of economic activity. A factory releases carbon, sulfur, heavy metals, and physical waste in the process of fabricating new tires, for instance. If permitted to dump some of these waste products in the local lake without repercussions, then the factory is producing a negative externality that impacts the lake and its ecosystem, as well as the human visitors who value the site in its clean, healthy state. But why not just call this "harm", since that is what it seems to be in essence? The reason is that economists try not to make moral judgments about distribution. They wish only to identify what counts as value and understand what choices can maximize this for people. The factory's pollution, under this amoral approach, is therefore simply a negative economic byproduct: it is considered a side-effect of the valuable production pursued by the factory. *Who* should bear the costs of these side-effects, much like who should get the benefit of profits generated, are not *per se* questions most economists would want to answer. Instead, they would prefer to send us to political scientists or philosophers. But for lawyers, the question of who should suffer harm or bear its costs has traditionally been the crux of legal disputes. The application of law in such instances, therefore, when negative externalities are identified and valued (in terms of costs), is usually intended to force the wrongdoer to take responsibility for what would otherwise be a cost easily passed on to others without accountability. Crime, under this approach, therefore, is considered economic activity for which negative externalities are high: a purse snatcher is taking advantage of the economic opportunity to appropriate another's handbag and passing the cost of this on to the victim. An embezzling financial advisor is taking the opportunity to make risky investments in their own name using client funds and passing the risk of loss to the client themself. By making theft and embezzlement codified crimes accompanied by scheduled punishments, legislatures are in a sense forcing would-be perpetrators to evaluate their economic incentives to conduct the theft or embezzlement in light of the fact that the negative externality either creates will necessarily be absorbed by the perpetrator themselves.

The second such role for criminal law from a Law and Economics perspective is to build or maintain confidence in market stability. In general lawyer-economists believe that efficient markets are usually the best medium through which goods and services should be distributed through a society. This means that resources are allocated to their highest-value positions when individuals and organizations are allowed to freely trade them in a competitive environment. But free trading in a competitive environment assumes that people will not cheat or harm one another in the process. Laws aimed at reducing crime are, in effect, rules to reduce cheating or harmful behavior that might make people hesitate to meet and transact in the marketplace. As already suggested, some activities called "crime" by the legislature are economic crimes that victimize asset holders to the benefit of perpetrators. Most financial frauds are of this nature. But then there are many more non-economic crimes, such as assault or kidnapping, that are even more discouraged. In all cases, reduction or prevention of crimes helps people in general feel safer, and it therefore supports their inclination to transact with one another in a market.

The third key role is to counter adverse distributional effects caused by criminal-type activities. In a world in which criminal-type activity were permissible, social goods would flow to those most in a position to threaten or coerce others: people with the largest stature, heaviest weaponry, or resources to hire others with the former two resources. The taking of goods by force in these ways would then shift the expense of those goods—in other words, the costs of losing them—to the victims. To an economist this is, as with the "negative externalities" above, a bad thing, even though morality is not the reason why. Criminal conduct creates a negative economic impact on victims to the benefit of perpetrators, and a strong criminal law helps to ensure those perpetrators are made to "feel" the negative effects of their own actions.

In order for criminal law to serve these roles, it must be able to exert control on people's behavior; here we see what is potentially the *most* important feature of criminal law and punishment: *deterrence*. Deterrence refers to any law or policy's ability to discourage people from doing something. The opposite term might be *incentives*—which conversely encourage people to take action. Deterrence and incentives are not unique to the criminal justice system. However, they are especially important within it; law enforcement would be vastly overwhelmed and ineffective if it had to individually enforce every rule against every would-be criminal actor. Indeed, in situations where the conduct is too commonplace—for instance, jaywalking—police must often choose not to enforce the law. So, with activities such as theft or financial fraud, law enforcement must rely on the deterrent quality of the rules themselves to discourage most people from participating.

Criminal law's deterrent function works in two important ways. On one hand, it takes advantage of the tendency, assumed in classical economics and in Law and Economics especially, for individuals to be opportunistic as "rational value maximizers". If a person is contemplating robbing a supermarket cash register, for instance, they are probably doing so with the understanding that the financial gains likely to result outweigh the risk of apprehension and punishment. The choice to rob is therefore—in this highly limited sense—"rational". But, the theory goes, if the punishment is made more severe and this is public information, would-be robbers now have to consider that the unlikely chance of apprehension would result in a greater loss of freedom and opportunity in the end. The risk calculation is tilted, and the rational-actor robber should refrain from committing the act.

On the other hand, it also counteracts the tendency for certain actors to want to conduct economic activity *outside* the market context. Just as the deterrent function discourages the harmful activity of robbery at a grocery cash register, it *encourages* individuals to find other more legitimate ways to obtain money. They must instead, the thinking goes, find a job in the legitimate economy. This may be speculative, since career criminals may not be able to find "legitimate" employment, and yet for other kinds of activity—for example black-market trading of scarce children's toys before Christmas—there is a more direct link: if people cannot buy things more cheaply from unregulated sources, most will buy them at the next lowest cost from licensed vendors. This, in turn, supports the efficiency of that market, directs income from sales tax to the authorities, and ensures proper warranties and product safety will remain in effect for those products entering the world.

Criminal law is one of the most important yet least understood grounds on which Law and Economics has been developed and applied. It relies at its base upon the deterrence function of legal rules, and works in the forgoing ways to strengthen markets even when its primary purpose appears to be public safety.

Administrative Law

A final legal subject area, and one particularly important in "public law", happens to be administrative law. Administrative law refers to the rules and regulations promulgated not by the courts, nor by national or state legislatures consisting of elected officials, but rather by executive agencies. An executive agency is a bureaucratic organization set up under the executive branch of government ostensibly for the purpose of enforcing "the law". And yet, as they are licensed to create their own regulations in pursuit of law enforcement, administrative agencies are in fact able to make laws in their own right.

A classic example is the United States Environmental Protection Agency (E.P.A.). The E.P.A. is only one of several "independent agencies" alongside the Civil Rights Commission and the Federal Communications Commission among others. Its independence means its director cannot be fired by the president, despite the fact that it sits under the ultimate authority of the chief executive. Following a formal procedure for draft publication, public comment, and adoption, the E.P.A. can therefore—for example—promulgate a rule protecting the endangered owl referenced above and limiting logging in select areas.

But, and this is perhaps the most significant development in administrative law under a Law and Economics influence, many administrative regulations since the 1980s must comply with a strict directive to meet a cost–benefit analysis test. In 1981, President Ronald Reagan signed Executive Order 12291 requiring that any new regulation with an effect on the economy amounting to $100 million or more would require that

> Regulatory action shall not be undertaken unless the potential benefits to society from the regulation outweigh the potential costs to society ... Regulatory objectives shall be chosen to maximize the net benefits to society [and] ... Among alternative approaches to any given regulatory objective, the alternative involving the least net cost to society shall be chosen.

This assessment of cost versus benefit would have to be undertaken by the proposing agency, and it would be submitted to the Office of Information and Regulatory Affairs (O.I.R.A.), a division of the Office of Management and Budget. Significantly, several of O.I.R.A.'s appointed executives over the years have been lawyers and judges. One, Cass Sunstein, who directed the office from 2009 to 2012 under President Obama—one of Sunstein's former students—is a highly cited lawyer-economist with a particularly behavioral outlook on the relationship between rules and economic choice. Although the cost–benefit oversight mandate of O.I.R.A. was developed under Reagan—perhaps the most deregulatory American president in memory—it was importantly renewed and relaunched under President Clinton in the 1990s and, of course, maintained under Obama. This distinctly utilitarian approach to regulation, therefore, has not been unique to partisan conservatives and has, rather, been adopted as part of a mainstream approach to policy in the United States.

Returning to environmental protection, the E.P.A. has been particularly hamstrung by the O.I.R.A. requirement to show greater net economic benefit "to society". Its rules tend to protect air, water, and soil, for which the consequences of pollution cannot be fully known

for decades or centuries, and it therefore has a difficult job when trying to show its benefits are "economically" beneficial in the short run.
According to one report, O.I.R.A. had altered more than 80 percent
of E.P.A. regulations in a ten-year period ending in 2011 (ProPublica
2014). Its efforts became the subject of substantial lobbying by anti-
environmental interests such as shipping giants FedEx and UPS, as well
as coal and chemical producers (2014).

Conclusion

This review of economic influences on key legal subject areas throws
into relief some of the large differences between what law is expected to
do and what it actually can do. The economic approach to legal rule-
making, enforcement, and adjudication makes efficiency a top priority
both in terms of using law's own resources, and in terms of maximizing
society's. It also illustrates the great influence Law and Economics has
had far beyond the legal academy where, we already know, it has been
profound. But it also raises more unanswered questions for the remainder of this book to explore.

For one thing, how might lawyer-economists negotiate what counts
as fact and what counts as opinion, or values? In his lifetime, Milton
Friedman, along with the Chicago School generally, was a proponent
of what Friedman called "positive economics"—that is to say the
description of the way the world *is*. It was, Friedman said, about *facts*.
Normative economics, a distinction he borrowed from Keynes' academic
father John Neville Keynes, was about values. Friedman felt the proper
role of economics was to study facts only; and yet, the legal application
of economic principles is, by its nature, a normative exercise. How then,
do lawyer-economists stretch the positive economics inherited from the
Chicago School and apply them in ever new permutations to new policies driven by the legal perspective on what society *should be*?

Next, and relatedly, what should be done about inequality? As the
decades wore on in the history of Law and Economics, this question
would become more pressing. The 1980s through the 2000s generally
saw economic growth and stability in the West. But the later 2000s
brought a great financial crisis followed by austerity and runaway social
inequalities; sure, there was more wealth in the system, but more income
was concentrated in fewer hands than at any point since the Great
Depression (Kelleher 2019). This crisis has given rise to a new "Law
and Political Economy" movement challenging traditional lawyer-economists who had said—with economists—that distributive choices were
not in their purview. As I have written elsewhere, however, several key
Law and Economics scholars have been concerned with inequality for

some time—even if they lacked the tools for studying why it was permitted in certain cases but not others (Tejani forthcoming).

And this gives rise to yet a third unanswered question. If inequalities have been tolerated and even encouraged through much legal-economic scholarship over the years, how do we explain societal aversions to market exchange and market-based distributions (the kind giving rise to inequalities in educational opportunity and health care)? These aversions are part of what Calabresi has called the moral "costs of costing" (2016, 131–2).

These outstanding issues of fact *vs.* value, inequality, and moral costs bring this discussion about Law and Economics back to a basic question: how did economics enter the study and practice of law in the first place, and what has happened as Law and Economics has grown more and more influential? The next chapter turns to these questions by examining the immediate "landscapes" into which Law and Economics entered, and on which it has exercised influence throughout the world.

References

Abraham, Kenneth. 2002. *The Forms and Functions of Tort Law*. 2nd ed. New York: Foundation Press.

Biasi, Marco, and Giovanni Tuzet. 2016. "From Judge-Made Law to Scholar-Made Law? The Strange Case of Employment-at-Will in the US." Available at SSRN: https://ssrn.com/abstract=3135813.

Blackstone, William. 1755. "Of Master and Servant," *Commentaries on the Laws of England*, Book 1., 413. Available at PROJECT GUTENBERG https://www.gutenberg.org/files/30802/30802-h/30802-h.htm#Footnote_E_990.

Calabresi, Guido. 2016. *The Future of Law and Economics*. New Haven, CT: Yale University Press.

Coase, Ronald. 1937. "The Nature of the Firm." *Economica* 16 (4): 386–405.

Coase, Ronald. 1960. "The Problem of Social Cost." *Journal of Law and Economics* 3 (October): 1–44.

Epstein, Richard A. 1984. "In Defense of the Contract at Will." *University of Chicago Law Review* 51: 947–982.

Frank, Robert. 2013. "Ronald Coase, a Pragmatic Voice for Government's Role." *New York Times*, September 14.

Friedman, Milton. 1970. "The Social Responsibility of Business Is to Increase Its Profits." *New York Times Magazine*, September 13, 122–126.

Kaplow, Louis. 1992. "Rules Versus Standards: An Economic Analysis." *Duke Law Journal* 42: 557–629.

Kelleher, Kevin. 2019. "Gilded Age 2.0: U.S. Income Inequality Increases to Pre-Great Depression Levels." *Fortune*, February 13. https://fortune.com/2019/02/13/us-income-inequality-bad-great-depression/.

Kolasky, William. 2020. "Aaron Director and the Origins of the Chicago School of Antitrust Part II—Aaron Director: The Socrates of Hyde Park." *Antitrust* 35 (1) (Fall): 101–106.

Leitzel, Jim. 2015. *Concepts in Law and Economics: A Guide for the Curious.* Oxford: Oxford University Press.

Locke, John. 1946 [1689]. *The Second Treatise of Civil Government*, John W. Gough ed., Oxford: Basil Blackwell.

Mauss, Marcel. 2000. *The Gift: The Form and Reason for Exchange in Archaic Societies.* New York: W.W. Norton and Co.

Medema, Steven. 2021. "Looks Can Be Deceiving: Ronald Coase and the Chicago School." *Promarket.org*, September 19. https://www.promarket.org/2021/09/19/ronald-coase-chicago-school-history/.

Mercuro, Nicholas, and Steven Medema. 1997. *Economics and the Law: From Posner to Post-Modernism and Beyond.* Princeton, NJ: Princeton University Press.

Posner, Richard. 1973. *The Economic Analysis of Law.* New York: Aspen Publishers.

ProPublica. 2014. "Lobbyists Bidding to Block Government Regs Set Sights on Secretive White House Office." *ProPublica.org*, July 31. https://www.propublica.org/article/lobbyists-bidding-block-government-regs-sights-set-secretive-white-house.

Schwartz, Pedro. 2013. "Ronald Coase, the Unexpected Economist." *EconLib.org*, October 7.

Tejani, Riaz. Forthcoming. "Calabresi's Invite: Law and Economics and the Problem of Situated Valuation."

Tejani, Riaz. 2019. *Law and Society Today.* Berkeley, CA: University of California Press.

Teles, Steven M. 2008. *The Rise of the Conservative Legal Movement.* Princeton, NJ: Princeton University Press.

Chapter 2

Landscapes

Introduction

So far, we have seen general themes behind Law and Economics and delved into some key ways in which they have affected private and public law since the mid-20th century. The approach has been primarily that of intellectual history, with a focus on ideas more than people or politics. This has allowed us to learn some of the vocabulary used in discussions about Law and Economics, and some of the main institutions which it has influenced. But ideas never exist in a vacuum; they emerge and develop in social and political contexts. And in this case, because economic perspectives on law influence the very notion of justice in society, we might say that Law and Economics emerged and developed in part to *change* its social and political contexts. And yet, as we will see, opinions about the direction such change should take can differ greatly among various experts in the field.

Law and Economics is colloquially known, especially among sociolegal scholars—sociologists and anthropologists of law among others—as part of a "conservative legal movement" (Teles 2008). Many of its most outspoken advocates and experts have indeed been connected to conservativism—by which I here mean a sociopolitical orientation that prefers minimal government control and support, smaller tax burdens, slower cultural change, and a primacy of business and commerce in society. How "conservatism" became known for these attributes is an interesting but separate question for another volume. Saying Law and Economics is connected to those values is to say that its writers have published papers supporting them, earned institutional positions at universities and think tanks associated with them, and even held judicial or regulatory appointments on the basis of their views about them.

And yet, it would be quite wrong to say that the whole movement is conservative. There is, in fact, a diversity of thought and opinion both about the relevance of conservative social and political priorities to Law and Economics, and about the social and political conclusions Law and

DOI: 10.4324/9781003350767-3

Economics leads to. This complexity is on display now more than ever. And yet, it is not new; rather, Law and Economics has oscillated slowly between progressive—by which I mean an orientation favoring government oversight and welfare support, increased legal rights for sociocultural minorities, and the importance of distributional justice—and conservative politics since its beginnings. The overarching claim of this chapter, then, is that Law and Economics has long experienced both progressive and conservative tendencies from within its ranks, and that these diverse sociopolitical orientations are identifiable in the history and scholarship produced by its key players.

Supporting that claim, this chapter first examines the emergence of Law and Economics during and after the Great Depression to reveal that the origins were not—by any stretch—strictly conservative. It then describes what many refer to as the "three waves" of modern Law and Economics thought. Here we will see that the periodicity and generational differences of each wave lead to shifting sociopolitical orientations. And then this chapter broaches a "new" issue not substantially considered elsewhere before: how has the movement's contact and encounter with the wider world, for instance through global legal education and transnational knowledge exchanges, reflected itself in the theory and research that Law and Economics engages in?

Emergence

In the fall of 1929, the world economy began a downward spiral that would continue for three years, and from which recovery would take nearly a decade. In late October that year, the U.S. stock market lost approximately 24 percent of its value almost overnight. Individual and institutional investors lost vast sums of money, and numerous firms were forced to lay off workers. Over the ensuing years, unemployment in the United States rose to roughly 23 percent, and gross domestic product fell by 15 percent. In other countries around the world, the situation was often much worse. Economists, especially, struggled to understand how this could happen.

Prior to this period, it was broadly thought in the United States that free enterprise was the most efficient and prosperous economic system available. Marxist ideology had already taken root in the new Soviet Union as of 1917, but that nation had specific conditions of underdevelopment and wide inequality that made its appeal stronger there than anywhere else to date. Recall, for example, that Marx was a German national who completed much of his writing in Paris and London. He was inspired greatly by the new British industrial economy in which factory workers suffered greatly at the hands of large business owners. This was something different than in Russia, where, as of 1917, roughly

83 percent of the population lived in rural areas and many of these were agricultural peasants. In other words, whereas a centralized command economy was embraced in the Soviet Union in the early 20th century, the absence of a large rural peasantry, the rapid growth of industrialization, and the high degree of urbanization in Western Europe and North America made it seem as though a free-market economy was successfully supporting rapidly growing populations.

And so, the stock market crash of 1929 came as a shock to most, even to economists. In hindsight, several causes were advanced regarding what might have caused the collapse. First, the commercial firms making up the Western economies had gotten very large. In the United States, the 1920s saw the culmination of the "robber baron" period in which several elite families attained and held much of the nation's wealth through several large conglomerate corporations. These included the Vanderbilts, the Rockefellers, and the Carnegies—all of whom have universities and colleges named for themselves to this day. The companies they owned included steel, coal, and railroad operations that had become the lifeblood and arteries of American industrialization. More importantly, several of these companies engaged in "vertical monopolies" in which they acquired and held firms at different stages of a production process. So, for example, a railroad company could acquire steel and coal operations and save on supply costs by sourcing raw materials "in house". The early 20th century saw considerable vertical integration of this kind, and this set up the conditions by which failure in one area of the economy could quickly spread to others. Moreover, this type of monopoly—along with "horizontal monopolies" in which one firm might buy out competitors and take over their operations—reduced open competition, later considered the lynchpin of a healthy market.

Furthermore, the growth of stock markets before 1929 was another important variable in the collapse. The advent of the publicly traded stock company—in which equity in a firm is divided up into hundreds, thousands, or even millions of "shares" and traded openly on a secondary market—had already existed since the 1602 creation of the Dutch East India Company and Amsterdam Stock Exchange. But industrialization and new technology, such as the electric stock ticker telegraph, made stock investments more widespread, faster, and more frenzied than they initially had been. Experts describe the type of investing taking place in this period (and others like it) as "speculation" because decisions to invest were made not on the relative strength of specific businesses but on a speculative presumption that the market indices would continue to rise simply because they always had. By 1929, ten percent of Americans held stocks and were exposed to risk when the market collapsed. Ultimately, however, the crash was just one contributor to the larger economic depression, since it was mostly through job and income loss that most people experienced the downturn of the next decade.

This was all possible because government regulation of large industries and of securities (of which stocks are but one type) exchanges was slow to catch up with rapid growth and integration. Indeed, the period prior to the Great Depression was considered something of a low point for government efforts to reduce the risks monopolies posed to market economy (Stucke and Ezrachi 2017). Many had believed that regulation and meaningful taxes were unnecessary because open markets would foster competition and better wealth redistribution (see Sowell 2012).

But the crash and the ensuing Great Depression naturally changed that opinion for many. For the first time in the West, as if to confirm some of the predictions made by Marx and his collaborator Friederich Engels, it appeared that capitalism was a broken system, or that it was no system at all but rather a dog-eat-dog race to accumulate more before the next crisis and scarcity. The popularity of Marxist ideas and organizations rose during the Depression as they appealed more to workers who suffered the worst precarity. But for professionals and economists who were more insulated, the problems of the period pointed not to Marx but to John Maynard Keynes. Keynes was the eccentric British economist who began publishing articles just after the 1929 crash and then completed his most famous text, *The General Theory of Employment*, in 1936. In these writings, Keynes argued that fully "free" markets were unstable and prone to regular downward cycles in between periods of growth. He theorized an important role for Western governments to erect "countercyclical" policies such as raising interest rates to blunt the impact of these downturns. This claim, that government regulation had an important role to play, not in owning or controlling key industries but in managing the flow of money and credit, led to the important realization that between "free markets" and "command economies" sat the more moderate middle way of state intervention in macro-economic policy. Which brings us, finally, to the institutional nascence of Law and Economics.

The "birth" of modern Law and Economics in the post-Depression era can be viewed from the perspective of both legal academia and legal "practice". In legal academia, by which I mean the discussions and debates around law taking place in and around universities and law schools, the groundwork for an interdisciplinary approach to law drawing on outside disciplines had already been laid by the American Legal Realist movement. Here, I refer to this as "Legal Realism" with the understanding that there was indeed also a Scandinavian Legal Realist movement occurring in roughly the same period early in the 20th century.

American Legal Realism began with several early calls for a socio-logical understanding of law "in action" contrary to, or complimentary with, the formalist approach already in practice among judges and aca-demics early in the 20th century. Legal formalism believed several key things about law: it could be found and read in published books; legal change to keep up with society could be charted using a "scientific" approach to jurisprudence; and legal education could be distilled into a "case method" approach in which students read and discussed court opinions to induce the rule as it evolved case-by-case. One of the key figures associated with the formalist trend in legal academia and educa-tion was Christopher Columbus Langdell. Langdell was appointed Dean of Harvard Law School in 1870 as a reformer; he was entrusted with the role of reforming the delivery of legal education in the law school toward a more engaged, dialectical relationship rather than the rote-lecture-and-memorization offered in the preceding decades. At that time in the American and English legal professions, when training took place mostly through apprenticeship in extant law firms, "law school" was not a required step toward becoming a lawyer. The Langdellian reforms were, in part, intended to distinguish the experience and training offered in a university setting from the mere practical iteration of legal educa-tion available more easily. It was, in other words, a way of making law school more distinct and elite. But Langdell's case method was seen as an extension, rather than a reform, of the formalist approach; it asked students to deduce rules by analyzing court cases almost exclusively. This meant that what counted as "law" in that environment was primar-ily case law. This reinforced an institutional approach to law in which power, social inequalities, and ethical disagreements were overlooked or muted.

In the period between World War I and World War II, an era marked in the United States by massive immigration and urbanization as well as by the economic collapse of the Great Depression, a group of American legal scholars grew weary of the formalist approach even as delivered by Langdell's case method. One was Oliver Wendell Holmes—an associate justice of the United States Supreme Court and professor at Harvard Law School. Holmes rejected the "natural law" school of thought holding instead that "the life of the law has *not* been logic, it has been experience" (Holmes 1991). This statement captures neatly Holmes' conviction that law cannot sit separate and apart from the social, political, and economic contexts in which it sits, and on which it exerts force. In approximately the same period, Roscoe Pound became Dean of the Harvard Law School and, from that position, advocated a realistic jurisprudence grounded in "human conditions" (1914). Pound himself was responsible for drawing the distinction between law-in-books versus law-in-action. Like the other Realists of the time, he was initially a strong supporter of the "New Deal"—a suite of government and legislative reforms designed to lift the United States out of the economic depression. In time, however, Pound split from the Realists as well as President Roosevelt's economic reforms. One reason was that he viewed several of the proposed changes, such as "court packing" the Supreme Court to dilute its oversight power, to be anti-democratic. Another reason was a bitter dispute with the Columbia law scholar and dean Karl Llewellyn. Llewellyn was another strong advocate of Realism in American academic law, but he also demonstrated how the realist approach could be implemented in both policy and research. In policy, Llewellyn used his extensive comparative and international experience in helping to reform the Uniform Commercial Code, bringing insights from the German legal tradition—which he read in its original, thanks to years spent studying in the country—and from indigenous North American legal practices related to exchange and disputing. The latter he had studied comprehensively and deeply in his collaboration with anthropologist E. Adamson Hoebel (Papke 1999).

The last decade of Llewellyn's life was spent at the University of Chicago, where he was on faculty until his death in 1962. This year is not insignificant: Coase's seminal "Problem of Social Cost" had been published in 1960 and its author joined the Chicago law faculty in 1964. Karl Llewellyn, along with the other Realists of the early 20th century, had very much paved the way for economists to legitimately analyze law from outside itself, using theory and methods cultivated in the social sciences. Llewellyn's presence at Chicago in the 1950s could be viewed as a strong indication of that law school's embrace of interdisciplinary methods, and it would foreshadow the rise of Chicago as the preeminent hub for Law and Economics after the 1960s. But neither was this rise inevitable. It came through the institution-building work of at least three people.

The University of Chicago became the center for American Law and Economics through the work of Henry Simons, Aaron Director, and arguably Henry Manne. None of these individuals was ever a scholastic "giant" in the field. Instead, it was their leadership and organizational work that distinguished their careers and built a "movement".

Without Henry Simons, Chicago Law and Economics would have had a much later start, if any. Simons joined the University's economics department in 1927 along with his mentor Frank Knight (Duxbury 1995, 335). But Simons' tenure in economics was lackluster and short-lived. It seems his scholarly output in that period was meager, and he was not well liked as a teacher. So, in 1939, a colleague arranged for Simons to teach a one-off course in the law school, which was well received and led to his promotion and tenure in 1942 (1995, 336). Although it is said that Simons did not make a substantial impact on his colleagues, "His appointment to the law school nevertheless marked the beginning of the Chicago law and economics tradition; for his writings provide a fairly clear indication of how that tradition would develop" (1995, 336). But whereas Chicago would soon come to be known for its price theory and small-government advocacy, Simons thought still bore the mark of Keynes (countercyclical intervention) more so than Hayek or Friedman (libertarian antistatism). As many have said, the start of Chicago Law and Economics came with a small, almost incidental effort to salvage the career of a struggling economist by moving him from the department of economics—where he would never receive tenure—to the law school.

The next major step came with the arrival and rise of Aaron Director. Russian-born Director attended graduate school in economics at Chicago in 1927 where he continued teaching on and off as an instructor for nearly 20 years. In 1945, Frederick Hayek secured a substantial sum of money to establish a center for the study of "free enterprise" at Chicago to be housed at the law school rather than in the economics department. Henry Simons recommended Director to serve as its first head, whereupon Director received a faculty appointment in the law school. From there, he would come to step into the teaching shoes of Simons, who passed away in 1946 (Duxbury, 1995, 342). Director's influence on Chicago Law and Economics was more deliberate, and more institutional than anything Simons had ever achieved. He founded the *Journal of Law and Economics*. He advocated both for the publication of Hayek's *Road to Serfdom* as well as his faculty appointment at Chicago. And he began a long process of teaching Chicago law students his unique neo-classical vision of law's role in economic governance. Federal appeals Judge Robert Bork who studied under Director at Chicago said, "A lot of us who took the antitrust course or the economics course underwent what can only be called a religious conversion. It changed our view of the entire world" (quoted in Teles 2008, 94).

Finally, another disciple of Director became the third key figure in the establishment of institutional Law and Economics. Henry Manne studied law at Chicago from 1949 to 1952. "I received my first serious introduction to libertarian views there", Manne said. "The man most responsible for my education in libertarian values was Aaron Director, the economist in the law school" (quoted in Teles, 2008, 104). After earning his undergraduate degree in economics at Vanderbilt, a law degree at Chicago, and L.L.M. at Yale, Manne joined the George Washington University law faculty where he made a mark publishing controversial papers on corporate law. Manne then was offered a position in political science at the University of Rochester. At Rochester, Manne collaborated intensively with the economics department and business school, and he developed a plan to launch an all-new law school rooted in free-market ideas and legal scholarship (Teles 2008, 102). Manne changed institutions twice more before finally being offered the opportunity to implement this plan for a libertarian-oriented law school at George Mason University. Throughout these moves, Manne developed several important programs that became central to Law and Economics leadership. One was the Economics Institutes for Law Professors started at Rochester, in which law faculty would be invited for a short residency during one of the academic breaks, and in which they would receive basic instruction in economic theory and methods. By his own estimate, these institutes taught over 650 law professors over the years (2008, 106). The faculty institutes later expanded to a separate judicial institute to which sitting state and federal judges were invited to teach the foundations of economic analysis of law. These judges moved on to draft court opinions bearing the mark of the Manne–Director approach to law in society—one that views justice through the lens of efficiency and the role of the State as a steward of "the market". Today, these institutes and a suite of related workshops are housed at George Mason's Law and Economics Center, and they continue to spread the message crafted by Manne.

In the years between Manne's departure from Rochester and his establishment of the George Mason Program, many of his program ideas were ultimately funded by the John Olin Foundation. Olin had been a multimillionaire industrialist who had built his fortune out of his father's chemical manufacturing company, then through the acquisition and growth of the Winchester rifle company. The charitable foundation created to disburse the family's massive fortune was founded in the early 1950s but remained largely a vehicle for laundering money for the C.I.A. In the 1970s, however, sparked by fears that Cornell University—Olin's alma mater—was being overrun with progressive values, Olin began a program of funding conservative projects within American higher education. One of its earliest grant recipients was indeed Henry Manne, who convinced the foundation that his Law and Economics Center would be a bastion of free-market, anti-regulatory, small-government ideas. Olin threw its support behind Manne, leading in turn to the well-funded faculty and judicial institutes named above. But Manne was almost too successful, and the Olin board of directors began to wonder why they should fund his work at places like Emory and Miami rather than people at more respected institutions such as Harvard and Yale. The Olin Foundation first moved in the 1970s to endow centers for the study of Law and Economics at U.S.C. and the University of Virginia (Teles 2008, 118). Economics at that time was still an exotic "Other"[1] to law, and the more elite law schools remained initially skeptical. But the influx of Olin money permitted these schools to hire new and higher impact faculty, as well as to create new joint-degree programs allowing J.D. candidates to pursue a master's or doctorate degree in economics simultaneously. Many of the U.S.C. faculty hired during this wave of funding were later poached by higher-ranked schools in subsequent years. This, and the fact that Olin had its ambitions for the very top, allowed it to gain a beachhead in the 1980s among the elite: Chicago, Yale, Harvard, and Stanford, all, in time, came to accept the foundation's money and establish Olin centers and professorships. Whereas the mere creation and work of these centers among the top four law schools is noteworthy, and indeed was seen as a counterweight to the then-powerful Law and Society movement evolved out of the Marxist-influenced Critical Legal Studies movement, their real success was in generating several generations of new students steeped in the Law and Economics tradition.

One of the key features of the "emergence" of Law and Economics as a legal academic subfield was its leadership. Henry Simons, Aaron Director, and Henry Manne are not remembered for their scholarship so much as for their entrepreneurial acumen. And yet, one must still ask the question: what value or values *motivated* this acumen in the first place? The first two were working adults during the Great Depression, while the latter came of age during it. All three saw the ways in which Keynesian economics pointed to increased government controls on economic, and thus social, life, and ultimately came to reject that approach in favor of what they believed better promoted human freedom. But the other key feature described in this section has been institution-building. People alone can only do so much to "build" movements. If they are fortunate, as Simons, Director, and Manne all were, resources emerge in the same moment that they are needed to support organization-building efforts. In a place such as North America, where, before the Internet, distances had to be bridged by social gatherings such as conferences, as well as the resources needed to travel, such support could not be overstated as a corequisite. Law and Economics found this support in the Olin Foundation, which would disburse some $370 million across all programs before its closure in 2005. The next section examines some of the key people forming this movement.

1 The term "Other" is common in cultural anthropology and refers to the structural opposite of relational identity. As Said famously wrote, European identity was forged out of opposition to the relational "Other" of the Near and Far East—a dynamic he called *Orientalism* (1978).

Figure 2.1 Geographic distribution of contemporary Law and Economics research centers in the United States. Three of these centers—Harvard, Yale, and Virginia—still bear the Olin family name.

The Three Waves

As we have seen, Law and Economics emerged thanks in part to the Legal Realists pushing for interdisciplinary and mixed methods studies of law as far back as the 1920s, in part to the economic crisis of the Great Depression and policy responses of the New Deal, and, finally, in part to the entrepreneurial institution-building of figures such as Simons, Director, and Manne. But as already suggested, these were merely conditions of possibility for the intellectual advances yet to come. Those advances came not in one large blast of inspiration, but rather in what many in Law and Economics still refer to as "waves". Waves are an interesting phenomenon in the natural world because they can behave in different ways at the same time. On one hand, they are defined as a "disturbance flowing through a medium" like the ocean waves one sees at the beach. But on the other hand, they can behave more like objects, both in the way they move together in batches, and in the way they come crashing ashore, capable of moving sand, eroding rocks, or smashing ships. Law and Economics is said to have progressed, so far, in three major "waves", and like their namesake in the natural world, these were similarly complicated and impactful.

The First Wave

The first wave of the subfield was necessarily its inaugural one, representing the period soon after Director arrived at Chicago and founded the *Journal of Law and Economics*. His faculty appointment took place in 1946, but the journal wasn't founded until 1953. In 1960 it published Ronald Coase's seminal "The Problem of Social Cost" which took issue with English economist Arthur Pigou's idea about the way externalities impacted economic welfare and necessitated compensatory justice. Pigou proposed the concept of externality and said that it was the role of the state to impose taxes on the beneficiaries to then redistribute to those harmed. Coase, as described in the previous chapter, argued that the market would solve such problems if, and only if, transaction costs could be reduced to near zero, and implied that courts need only make decisions (in other words establish conditions) that would approximate such a scenario. It was arguably with this seminal claim, which was, in an earlier form, rejected by members of the nascent Chicago School, that the so-called First Wave began. But what makes it a wave is not necessarily the substance of what Coase said, nor even the fact that he was able to convince a few important academics at that time. It started a "wave" because of the many new academics and intellectuals that it swept up into its forward movement. Of those, many would extend the implications of Coasian thinking into new terrain. None was more important in that regard than Richard Posner.

When one speaks about the origins of Law and Economics in the post-Depression American New Deal, one of the most important features of this was U.S. Department of Justice's antitrust work to ensure competitive markets. Some (Teles 2008) have asserted that antitrust law was the foothold with which Law and Economics established itself in the legal academy. In some ways, it was a safe ground on which liberal professors and conservative lawyers could meet eye-to-eye. Richard Posner's early role in the "first wave" is strong evidence for this. Posner graduated top of the class from Harvard Law School in 1962, at which point he joined the U.S. Federal Trade Commission. He then moved on to the Office of the Solicitor General, one of the highest-ranking offices in the Department of Justice, and there he handled antitrust cases for the government. Up to this point, Posner was, like most elite-trained U.S. lawyers, a liberal, and his boss at the Solicitor General's Office was Thurgood Marshall, the soon-to-be first African American Associate Justice of the Supreme Court. But while handling antitrust cases, Posner began a transformation toward viewing justice in essentialist economic terms. In 1968 he joined the Stanford Law Faculty where he met Aaron Director and George Stigler, whom he described as major influences; and the following year he moved to the University of Chicago where he remained affiliated well beyond his appointment to the federal bench by President Reagan in 1981.

Posner is unique in his professional profile and influence. His career began in the executive branch of government, transitioned to academia, then transitioned back to government, this time in the judiciary. In this regard, he exemplified an approach to legal theory and scholarship that is both practical and simple on one hand, and cogent and erudite on the other. In one of his key writings, for example, Posner rereads the famous 1947 Torts case U.S. *v. Carol Towing*—a case about a loose barge that broke free of its mooring in New York Harbor near the end of World War II and smashed into a pier and sank. The original opinion was authored by Justice Learned Hand for the Second Circuit Court of Appeals in New York. The issue at hand was, essentially, whether the barge owner was negligent in equipping the barge with a part-time pilot only. To answer this, Hand wrote that the answer depended upon a comparison between costs associated with manning the barge around the clock and the costs associated with the harm that could result from not doing so, multiplied by the probability of that harm materializing. Posner, writing in the early 1970s, took Hand's analysis of the negligence question, and distilled and amplified it; he argued in effect that what Hand was doing in 1947 was early Law and Economics, and that this type of reasoning was already prominent albeit latent in the common law itself stretching back to medieval England. Published in his now-seminal *Economic Analysis of Law* (1973), this simplification of common-law negligence into a form of Utilitarian cost–benefit analysis has become a classic: it repackaged an extremely large and complicated ethical theory into an easy modular formula which could be propagated to judges across American courtrooms and legitimated in terms of Western legal history. Using a similar structure, Posner would proceed to conduct economic analysis of numerous other legal subfields including family law, sex and gender law, law and literature, and more. This intellectual interloping sparked responses from native scholars in each field, only widening the debates into which Law and Economics had crept. But as Posner rode the "first wave" to significant notoriety—enough to earn an appellate court appointment—his closest equal was similarly influential for a more sober and philosophical approach.

Guido Calabresi, like Posner, was appointed to the Court of Appeals after a storied career as law school academic and dean. Unlike Posner, Calabresi's undergraduate training was in economics (though notably neither held terminal degrees in the field); he further distinguished himself by earning a Rhodes Scholarship and obtaining a second bachelor's from Oxford University. On his return, he completed a law degree at Yale, graduated first in his class, and joined the chamber of Supreme Court Justice Hugo Black. Offered a faculty position at Chicago, Calabresi declined that offer to instead join the Yale Law faculty as the youngest professor in the school's history, where he rose to dean in the 1980s. Unlike Posner, whose encounters with early Law and Economics pulled him in the direction of market fundamentalism via the Chicago School, Calabresi has remained a progressive scholar and judge. His influential writings do not point to a market-based solution to legal problems; they rather organize and reclassify existing legal questions into new and revealing categories and units. In 1972, for instance, he published with Douglas Melamed, "Property Rules, Liability Rules and Inalienability: One View of the Cathedral", in the *Harvard Law Review*. The article took up the difference between property law and tort law solutions to various types of disputes. Property, the authors point out, comes with inherent rights to use and enjoy on the part of owners and occupiers of land. The allocation or reallocation of those rights can serve to remedy a situation where one person's use of their land might interfere with another's different use of theirs. Such rights can also be bought and sold, and therefore allow the kind of bargaining and trading Coase had theorized in his "Problem of Social Cost". But tort disputes—car accidents, for example—are treated differently because, as the last chapter said, bargaining around rights is too slow to prevent harm from occurring in the first place. In other words, one could theoretically pay other drivers to buy their right to safe road use so that they might speed at 95 miles per hour, but drivers are not typically in a position to transact with other drivers on the road while driving. For this situation, the law employs "liability rules" which, in effect, impose damage costs on the speeding driver after the fact. Under property rules, the transaction between parties is supposed to be voluntary, whereas for liability rules it is involuntary.

This distinctive framing led to several new implications. One was that, for scholars interested in law and inequality, a person with sufficient means—in other words someone very rich—could engage in tortious or even criminal behavior with the a priori understanding that he or she would simply pay the damages or fine if caught afterwards. In that regard, a poor person's liability rule was a wealthy person's property rule. But another implication was that the types of legal remedies available in one type of case could vary according to the means available to the parties. Taking, for instance, a nuisance-type case in which one land user was creating pollution that hampered the use and enjoyment of its neighbor, the remedies available for a court to apply already included: 1) a property rule enjoining (e.g., stopping harmful use by) the polluter; 2) a liability rule requiring the polluter to pay damages to the neighbor; or 3) a second property rule finding no nuisance at all and allowing the polluter to continue unabated. Calabresi and Melamed then predicted the feasibility of a "fourth rule"—a liability rule in which the court allows the polluter to carry on unobstructed *unless* the neighbor wishes to pay damages to enjoin the activity. This analysis showed the academic world that Law and Economics could be used to reorganize legal theory to predict new potential outcomes, and that some of those could be market-based in a way that supported Coase's assertion that courts try to simulate efficient market solutions when transaction costs are too high to allow them to develop "naturally".

Another key idea emergent in the work of Calabresi is the need for substantially more reflection in Law and Economics on the moral implications of economic choices. In his 1978 book with Phillip Bobbit, Calabresi raises the idea of "tragic choices" in which societies must allocate scarce resources in ways, and according to logics, that frequently must leave some without life-sustaining resources (Calabresi and Bobbit 1978). Some societies make such choices according to "command" (e.g., socialism) and others, including the United States and Western Europe, according to "the market". But there are unspoken moral costs to applying prices to certain social goods such as care, love, empathy, and so forth. Revisiting this in 2018, Calabresi refers to this as the "cost of costing" and says it is particularly acute in the domain of "merit goods"—the kinds of goods that make communities most uncomfortable with pricing. The implications of this line of thinking are, especially for sociolegal scholars and students, profound. Most of Chicago School economics is founded upon "price theory" or the notion that economic efficiency can be defined in terms of finding a price equilibrium when supply and demand are evenly matched. This implies that most things are capable of pricing, and that price is a good proxy for the health of an economy. But it also implies that economists assume away the mutually agreed valuation of whatever they are worried about maximizing. Calabresi, in his "costs of costing" and "merit goods" discussions, draws keen attention to several of the necessary assumptions that make Law and Economics so easy. He calls for a more anthropological accounting for the way human tastes actually shape choices about allocative systems, and about disparate valuations across them, and these ideas sit right at the frontier between law, economics, and social anthropology.

The Second Wave

Some of the problems identified by Calabresi about unstated assumptions among lawyer-economists started to receive attention in the 1980s from a new generation of experts with a different depth of training and research experience. This group, later known as "Second Wave Law and Economics", consisted of new J.D./Ph.D.s holding terminal degrees in both fields—rather than jurists with a little underlying economics training. The differences this group represented were stark. Ph.D.'s would have been required to produce original empirical research in economics, using existing datasets or gathering new ones. They would also be exposed to a wider variety of economic theories, including Marxist ones shunned by the Chicago School but still current in much of the world. And they would be interested in going beyond the mere "application" of economics to law. Calabresi underscores the latter by distinguishing the First Wave's "economic analysis of law" or E.A.L.—typified by Posner's extension of economic theory into virtually everything—from the Second Wave (and beyond) in its more mutually reflexive project to advance *both* legal and economic theory and concepts in what he calls true "Law and Economics".

So, the first key characteristic of the Second Wave is the "empirical turn". If it was made possible by the rise of dual-degree lawyer-economists, this was in turn made possible in part by money from the Olin Foundation. Recall that the conservative funding source sponsored Law and Economics centers at most of the elite law schools for two main purposes. One was to attract high-impact and fast-rising economics faculty to law schools, but the other was to generate new dual-degree programs that could offer a Ph.D. to promising law students. By the late 1980s, both goals were being achieved, and the scholars they produced would comprise much of the Second Wave. Louis Kaplow is one early figure of this branch in Law and Economics. Trained at Harvard Law School, he completed the J.D. in 1981 and Ph.D. in economics in 1987. He joined the Harvard faculty in 1982 and served as the Associate Director of the Olin Center there. Whereas the First Wave scholars took basic Chicago economics and applied them in theory to legal institutions such as property and tort rules, Kaplow was among the early empiricists who took on taxation, antitrust, and welfare using economic research methods. Like many later Ph.D.-trained lawyer-economists, Kaplow joined the National Bureau of Economics Research (N.B.E.R.), an ostensibly non-partisan non-profit economics think tank that issues working papers and consults on government and private projects.

Also active with N.B.E.R., the Yale Law and Economics scholar Ian Ayres is another figure emblematic of the Second Wave. After earning a J.D. from Yale in 1986 and an economics Ph.D. from M.I.T. in 1988, Ayres clerked at the Tenth Circuit Court of Appeals and taught at a series of elite institutions before rejoining Yale in the 1990s, where he remains today. Possibly more than any other Second Wave scholar, Ayres is also a prolific public intellectual authoring op-eds for *Forbes*, *NPR*, and *The New York Times* on topics ranging from gun violence, gender and race discrimination, and investment strategies. Based on even a cursory reading of Ayres' articles and opinion pieces, it is also clear that Ayres—like Calabresi—defies the stereotype many have of lawyer-economists as a "conservative" group. Ayres' biography on the Yale Law School website, for example, uses only the pronoun "they", and Ayres has published at least one opinion piece justifying this choice.

Whereas Kaplow and Ayres can be described as polymath in their choice of legal and economics subject matter, Eric Talley of Columbia Law School has been long focused on corporate law and governance. Talley earned a J.D. and an economics Ph.D. from Stanford in the 1990s where his advisors included Ian Ayres and Mitch Polinksy. In 1995 he joined the U.S.C. Law School, which hosted one of the early Olin centers for Law and Economics. There Talley became Director of the U.S.C.–Caltech joint Ph.D.-granting program in Law and Economics. From U.S.C., Talley would hold positions with the RAND Corporation and visiting positions with several law schools before moving on to Berkeley and then Columbia.

And finally, despite the prevailing profile of Law and Economics as a predominantly white and male profession in the United States, Christine Jolls of Yale Law School is a fourth key figure in the Second Wave. Trained in law at Harvard and in economics at M.I.T., she holds both terminal degrees and directs the Law and Economics program at N.B.E.R. Whereas Jolls writes on administrative and employment law, her greatest impact has been in the domain of Behavioral Law and Economics. There, she teaches a course on rational choice with Amartya Sen at Yale, and she has coauthored several key papers with Cass Sunstein.

These four scholars are indicative of the turn in Law and Economics later termed the Second Wave. They reflect several key features of their period in the subfield. One was a growing demand for dually trained doctoral degree holders who could not only *apply* economics to law but also conduct empirical studies while refining economic theory based on new insights. Another was recruitment from universities and departments farther afield than Chicago—albeit still elite institutions. A third development was new participation from ideologically progressive—or at least non-conservative—junior scholars. A fourth was openness to questioning some key assumptions that had characterized Chicago—most notably rational-actor theory—as seen in the rise of Jolls and her coauthors doing behavioral research. Fifth, and finally, Jolls herself, still the only woman among the top 15 most-cited lawyer-economists, does mark the beginning of a slow gender and ethnic diversity expansion that began in the 1990s and continues to this day in American Law and Economics.

Amid that push for greater demographic and methodological diversity (e.g., psychology, behaviorism), Law and Economics has also experienced a greater intellectual diversity that now includes scholars trained in economics *and* law, but is explicitly self-reflexive about the very power and inequality perpetuated by theories in economics and law. This new generation of scholars comprise what some have recently been calling the "Third Wave", and they are motivated in part by a growing interest in *political economy* within law. Here, political economy refers to the interplay and interchangeability of economic choices and political control. In the past, particularly during the Scottish Enlightenment of the 18th and 19th centuries, economics was viewed as deeply intertwined with politics, and the key economic thinkers of the period, including Adam Smith, Thomas Malthus, and David Ricardo, all wrote at the boundary between politics and economics. In general, they understood that policy choices, including electoral, legislative, and juridical ones, would have different economic implications and that economic winners and losers would have different political interests and demands from their leadership. The classical economists embraced this relationality; but the rise of Marxism in the East had the effect of discrediting political economy in the West. Marx was—like the classical thinkers—a political economist *par excellence*; his theory of capitalism as a totalizing system that would concentrate power among the few while expanding to convert the many into laborers, was certainly an argument at the apex of politics and economics. In part because of this association, and in part thanks to a simple anti-Keynesian consensus building around Chicago that the State did not belong in market activity, First Wave lawyer-economists had eschewed the "political economy" approach despite working, themselves, at the apex of economic value and judicial and regulatory policymaking on the other.

The Third Wave

Today's Third Wave lawyer-economists are far less reactive. They study the tax system to identify ways in which low-income citizens fail to apply for many of the benefits designed by elite lawmakers to help them. Jacob Goldin is a paradigmatic example of this new approach. In recent years, his writings have explored, in particular, the Child-Tax Credit established under U.S. law to permit parents to deduct standard amounts for every child, and Goldin and coauthors have shown that poorer families do not benefit from this provision as much as their middle-class counterparts (2022a, 2022b). This concern about inequality is a running theme for this new wave. Zachary Liscow, for example, has written extensively about the limitations of "efficiency" in Law and Economics in promoting distributional justice. "[E]fficient policies", Liscow writes, "are probably biased toward the rich. That is, in many cases … one of the dominant paradigms in the law is biased against the poor, which is a particular concern given rising dissatisfaction with economic inequality" (Liscow 2018, 1652).

Both Goldin and Liscow resemble the Second Wave scholars in that each was trained at the doctoral level in economics and J.D.-level in law. Both obtained their legal training at Yale Law School, and Liscow teaches there. In this regard, they also bear apparent influence from the earlier "New Haven School" in Law and Economics which began to embrace problems in distribution and inequality as early as the 1960s.

This recap of first-, second-, and third-wave lawyer-economists has focused deliberately (if reluctantly) on scholars from elite institutions. By far outnumbered by their counterparts at lower-ranked institutions, these writers may be more significant in their influence and impact. But influence and impact—particularly in an intellectual "movement"— require disciples. It is standard wisdom in U.S. academic law that scholars among the elite schools, especially ones appointed to such institutions early in their careers, will gain a bigger audience simply by virtue of institutional deference. In this regard, the United States is a microcosm for the world at large. U.S. lawyer-economists have thus been able to exert considerable influence on Law and Economics globally, and it is to this subject that the final section of this chapter now turns.

Pathways to the World

Thinking of American Law and Economics in (at least) three waves is salient for severeal reasons. One is that it is already how experts in the field—some of whom are quite old in age at this juncture and were present nearly at the inception—historicize themselves. Second, it allows us to periodize the development of these scholars, their ideas, and their impact on the world around them. And finally, it promotes a view of their activities in a larger academic and intellectual ecosystem. Like "waves" on a pond, we can envision certain moments of impact like a stone cast upon the surface disturbing the accepted calm and rippling outward in growing circles that ultimately reach the shoreline. Some shorelines are near, as in the influence of the New Haven school in places such as New York or Washington, D.C., and others are far—over the ocean on other continents. American Law and Economics, I suggest in this last section and in the following chapter, has dramatically impacted shorelines far afield. It has done so for two large reasons.

To start with, the impact of U.S. scholars in most fields has often tended to have global reach. For better and for worse, English has become a *lingua franca* for academics in S.T.E.M., Humanities, Social Sciences, and Law. U.S. journals, thanks to online access and digital repositories, are read widely now in other countries. And non-English journals are frequently co-published in both the native language and English simultaneously. At the same time, U.S. universities carry considerable reputational strength in most other parts of the world, and U.S. scholars have been disproportionately awarded for their discoveries in all of the major Nobel Prize categories since that institution was created. To date, U.S. scholars have claimed 403 Nobel awards, whereas the next nearest country, the United Kingdom, has received 137. In economics, the Nobel has only been awarded since 1968. Since that year, 92 scholars have received the award—some alongside one or more others in a given year. Of these 92 recipients, 68 claim the United States as either one of their home countries, or as their sole home. So, roughly 74 percent of all Nobel Prizes awarded in economics have gone to "American" scholars. Such numbers are not guarantors of any qualitative impact per se, but they serve as a proxy for high-level influence and reputational standing. For a more qualitative case study on economics, one need only review the role Milton Friedman and the Chicago School played in the economic policies of Latin America during the 1960s and 1970s. In that period, dozens of students were invited to Chicago with funding from the Ford and Rockefeller Foundations to study under its economics faculty in price theory and markets. Most of these students returned to Chile where they took up positions in the administration of dictator Augusto Pinochet—who had taken power by military coup and assassination of the democratically elected President Salvador Allende—and denationalized the nation's industries through Friedman-inspired liberalization policies. Indeed, at his Nobel Award ceremony, Friedman was interrupted by a Chilean protester shouting, "down with capitalism, freedom for Chile!"

And while there is no such global prize awarded in Law, other direct evidence suggests a similar latent deference afforded to U.S. legal scholars in the global arena. American constitutional scholars such as Erwin Chemerinsky and Noah Feldman have been called upon to help draft the constitutions of newly democratized nations in the East. Invitations to American legal scholars to teach in Europe and the Near East, especially Israel, are very common, and the establishment of Law and Economics institutes in the image of the Olin Centers at universities around the world has been rapid. To date, there are such centers at the University of Bologna in Italy, Sciences Po and the University of Paris in France, University College London in the UK, the University of Hamburg in Germany, Gujarat National Law University in India, Hokusei Gakuen University in Japan, and the Royal University of Law and Economics in Cambodia to name just a select few. American academics are frequently invited as visiting faculty to these institutions and are proud to say so on their institutional webpages.

But by far one of the largest influences on global Law and Economics theory and practice has come through the market for international LL.M. programs and degrees. Mindie Lazarus-Black and Julie Globokar noted a 50 percent rise in U.S. LL.M. programs from 1998 to 2003, leading to 179 such programs by 2007 (2015, 5). They also note that the international students populating these programs are *not* all from elite socio-economic backgrounds but rather from a growing middle-class segment present in developing countries (2015, 16–17). With the onset of the Great Recession and U.S. law school admissions decline around 2010, many schools also embraced the LL.M. as a "survival strategy". Later, under pressure for "diversity, equity, and inclusion" (D.E.I.), some schools also hailed LL.M. students as part of their institution's D.E.I. profile.

But the rise of the U.S. LL.M. in the global legal credentialing arms race is not, by far, solely a function of the demand for American social capital on one hand, nor the diversity and "cash cow" needs of U.S. institutions on the other. It is also, as Bryant Garth points out, the result of a willful search for global hegemony (2015). With the support of the U.S. State Department and public higher education authorities, LL.M. programs create cadres of American-influenced foreign attorneys and judges steeped in the Western common-law legal tradition, and sympathetic to U.S. international law and foreign policy priorities. Garth aptly connects this self-reflexive development of international networks to the same process that occurred in economics decades earlier:

The United States extends its influence and hegemony more from the export of its governing expertise—law but also economics in particular—as universal and modern. The export of economics as a governing expertise was characteristic of the Cold War as a way to influence mostly authoritarian governments to open their markets while serving as allies against communism. Well-known examples include the "Chicago boys" in Chile and the "Berkeley Mafia" in Indonesia, but the same process with economics is evident in South Korea, India, and elsewhere.

(2015, 71)

The connections drawn here, between international knowledge production in law and in economics, are compelling. Reflecting back on the nexus of politics and economics evidenced in classical economics, in Marxist political thought, and in today's Law and Political Economy group, it is clear that both law and economics sit adjacent to, and in feedback with, political influence and institutions. But what about explicit U.S. LL.M. programming in "Law and Economics" itself? Such programs exist currently at George Mason, Stanford, and Georgetown, while related "master of laws" programs with economics concentrations exist at U.S.C. and Arizona. Beyond these freestanding focused programs for existing attorneys, many of the remaining general LL.M.'s in the United States allow their international students to take Law and Economics coursework as part of their degree-completion requirements.

Conclusion

The story of Law and Economics has been one of an intellectual movement with a tangible origin, development, and institutional dominance. In this fashion, it has followed a somewhat linear path with identifiable "moments" of great progress and forward expansion. As described here, the origin story begins with the Great Depression and its impact on economic theory, followed by the New Deal policy response and its emphasis on antitrust law—which we now know furnished a pathway by which "economic analysis of law" could enter mainstream academic law. From that point forward, Law and Economics had its strongest base in Chicago where it grew in concert with the power and influence of the Chicago School, some of whose adherents were among the most successful institutional entrepreneurs in American higher education. Henry Simons, Aaron Director, and Henry Manne are names not regularly associated with big theoretical contributions, but instead with creating the structure that would come to house and support the many writers and teachers who advanced the subject intellectually.

Our brief look at Olin Foundation support added a material dimension to this story: how, but for the benefaction of a large private grant-funder, could even the most compelling academic movement access the resources necessary to spread its ideas far and wide? In concert with this financial backing, we saw that Law and Economics scholarship, viewed from the inside as well as the outside, progressed in three big "waves"; through this progression, we saw a shift from application of baseline economic theory "to" law toward empirical study of legal phenomena using economic methods, and an openness to refine economic theory as a result. At the same time, we noted a shift in political ideology from the conservative and libertarian tendencies of Manne and the later Posner toward the progressive social welfarist tendencies of Ayres, Liscow, and Goldin among others. Importantly, this progression was not exactly linear either: Coase produced early work on command structures, Simons was notably Keynesian in the early days, and Posner had been a high-ranking officer in Thurgood Marshall's Justice Department.

Finally, this chapter noted the international reputation and influence of many lawyer-economists stemming from what Bryant Garth has since identified as the hegemonic quality of American economics and law, as well as from a global demand for U.S. expertise as the world's financial system became more interconnected and instantaneous on the model of American Wall Street. The rise of the international LL.M. programs was a function of this twofold buildup in supply and demand, and they may in fact be the single most palpable avenue by which U.S. Law and Economics thought has entered the policy lexicon of the wider global financial system.

Putting all of this together, we see that Law and Economics expanded not only vertically in power and depth but also horizontally in scope and impact. This horizontal expansion, it can be said, has caused American Law and Economics—grounded in Anglo-Saxon classic political-economy—to encounter and be challenged by alternative economic, legal, and especially moral systems around the world. Indeed, if the Chicago School was known for essentializing "rational choice" as the measure of reasonable conduct and "efficiency" as the measure of justice, the expansion of the Law and Economics landscape across the globe has forced these ideas to answer questions from the legal cultures of India, China, the Middle East, and Latin America, among others. One keen example of this could be found in the story of Islamic banking, which flouts several of the key conventions in Western finance and law by institutionalizing an idea of justice that promotes greater fairness and equity (Maurer 2005). While this is just one easy example, the larger question to keep in mind is this: the more Law and Economics travels into "other" economic and legal cultures (and, therefore, value systems), how might social sciences and humanities help understand any new conflicts of translation or worldview it creates?

Surveying recent contributions from anthropology and sociology, three concepts come to mind in this regard: ontology, multi-perspectivity, and moral economy. Ontology, or more simply the study of how "reality" is shaped, was a major area of interest in Anthropology in the

2000s, and its influence will remain for some decades. It came—partly out of globalization and increased cultural and ethical contact world-wide—from the increased frequency of conflicts between various lived realities in a rapidly accelerating world. Why accelerating? Because the speed of travel (e.g., aircraft), communications (e.g., fiber optics, com-puting), and commerce (e.g., financial technologies) seemed to make the world smaller but cultural values bigger, or more consequential. Some examples of these heightened consequence include the debates and ban-ning of the Islamic headscarf in France (Scott 2004), the pressure of World Bank "structural adjustment" in Asia and Latin America (Paley 2001), anti-bribery penalties for European and South American mul-tinational corporations using the U.S. Foreign Corrupt Practices Act (Koehler 2012), and the rise of American Supreme Court litigation over human rights abuses by oil companies in Africa under the Alien Tort Statute (Hoffman and Zaheer 2003). In each case, the stability of an economic, legal, and moral "reality" was challenged by the collision of two or more value systems, and only one—usually the more powerful—would be allowed to prevail.

Relatedly, out of ontology comes the idea of "multi-perspectivity". In truth, this is a concept that long predates the "ontological turn" in the human sciences, but many returned to the classic writers such as Weber, Goffman, and Geertz to write about the way that what most consider "facts" are subject to interpretation from the moment of their discovery. In the mid-2010s, after decades of popularity in the academic universe, both ontology and multi-perspectivity would reappear in politics and journalism with the rise of "fake news", a phrase associ-ated with informational bubbles and echo chambers prior to the 2016 U.S. election. There, with the hardening of separate Left- and Right-leaning news sources—and including the rise of crowdsourced news on social media—the ability for American, and indeed global, society to agree upon shared "facts" declined considerably. But this same process allowed for political, religious, sexual, and ethnic minorities to reas-sert unpopular versions of accepted histories. Multi-perspectivity, like so many large interpretive ideas, was a double-edged sword.

And finally, the encounter of American Law and Economics with diverse legal cultures of the globe brought greater attention to the need for understanding moral economies. "Moral economy" was a concept developed famously by E.P. Thompson in work about the English work-ing class in the 18th century. Thompson used it to theorize the way in which even "hard" economic systems, comprised of production, distri-bution, and consumption, are, in fact, laden with moral choices—or at least the mark that such choices leave on the societies that make them. This concept would find echoes, I suggest, in the writings of Guido Calabresi on "the cost of costing" and "merit goods" a century later, and it should underpin any meaningful exploration of Law and Economics by social and human scientists today. When a lawyer-economist uses highly technical theory and method to argue that the benefits to society of some new economic policy outweigh the costs, and that the distribution of those benefits is, in effect, irrelevant, we can be sure that there are "moral" assumptions underpinning this argument, whether they are spoken or muted. Thompson's idea of a "moral economy" is, thus, essential to a critical understanding of Law and Economics.

Ontology, multi-perspectivity, and moral economy are social and human science concepts invoked by reflecting on American Law and Economics' migration into the wider world and its sociocultural diversity. The next chapter takes this reflection even further by examining the role played by Law and Economics in economic globalization, and in its ideological corollary—often called *neoliberalism*.

References

Calabresi, Guido, and Phillip Bobbit. 1978. *Tragic Choices: The Conflicts Society Confronts in the Allocation of Tragically Scarce Resources.* New York: W.W. Norton and Co.

Duxbury, Neil. 1995. *Patterns of American Jurisprudence.* Oxford: Oxford University Press.

Garth, Bryant. 2015. "Notes Toward an Understanding of the U.S. Market in Foreign LL.M. Students: From the British Empire and the Inns of Court to the U.S. LL.M." *Indiana Journal of Global Legal Studies* 22 (1): 67–79.

Goldin, Jacob. 2022a. "Whose Child? Designing Child-Claiming Rules for Safety Net Programs." *131 Yale Law Journal* 1719: 1719–1793 (2022) (with Ariel J. Kleiman).

Goldin, Jacob. 2022b. "Tax Filing and Take-Up: Experimental Evidence on Tax Preparation Outreach and Benefit Claiming." *Journal of Public Economics* 206 104550 (2022) (with Tatiana Homonoff, Rizwan Javaid & Brenda Schafer).

Hoffman, Paul L., and Daniel A. Zaheer. 2003. "The Rules of the Road: Federal Common Law and Aiding and Abetting Under the Alien Tort Claims Act." *Loyola L.A. International and Comparative Law Review* 26: 47–88.

Holmes, Oliver Wendell. 1991. *The Common Law.* New York: Dover Publications.

Koehler, Mike. 2012. "The Story of the Foreign Corrupt Practices Act." *The Ohio State Law Journal* 73 (5): 929–1013.

Lazarus-Black, Mindie, and Julie Globokar. 2015. "Foreign Attorneys in U.S. LL.M. Programs: Who's In, Who's Out, and Who They Are." *Indiana Journal of Global Legal Studies* 22 (1): 3–65.

Liscow, Zachary. 2018. "Is Efficiency Biased?" *Chicago Law Review* 85: 1649–1718.

Maurer, Bill. 2005. *Mutual Life Limited: Islamic Banking, Alternative Currencies, Lateral Reason.* Princeton, NJ: Princeton University Press.

Nowrasteh, Alex. 2022. "Immigrants Reduce Unionization in the United States." *Cato at Liberty*, June 28. https://www.cato.org/blog/immigrants-reduce-unionization-united-states.

Paley, Julia. 2001. *Marketing Democracy: Power and Social Movements in Post-Dictatorship Chile.* Berkeley, CA: University of California Press.

Papke, David. 1999. "How the Cheyenne Indians Wrote Article 2 of the Uniform Commercial Code." *Buffalo Law Review* 47 (3): 1457–1486.

Pound, Roscoe. 1914. "Justice According to Law." *The Mid-West Quarterly* 1 (3): 223–235.

Said, Edward. 1979. *Orientalism.* New York: Vintage Books.

Scott, Joan Wallach. 2004. *The Politics of the Veil.* Princeton, NJ: Princeton University Press.

Sowell, Thomas. 2012. *Trickle Down Theory and Tax Cuts for the Rich.* Stanford, CA: Hoover Institution Press.

Stucke, M.E., and A. Ezrachi. 2017. "The Rise, Fall, and Rebirth of the U.S. Antitrust Movement." *Harvard Business Review*, December 15.

Teles, Steven. 2008. *The Rise of the Conservative Legal Movement.* Princeton, NJ: Princeton University Press.

Chapter 3

Globalization

Introduction

The landscape in which Law and Economics emerged had a significant influence on how and where it would develop. We saw that this landscape included historic world events and policy responses founded on the prevailing and insurgent economic theories of the day. But through its growth and flourishing, the Law and Economics movement also substantially transformed the landscape around itself. In the previous chapter I flagged the global reach of this movement through internationally networked scholarship and through the birth and development of purposefully international Master of Law (LL.M) programs. This chapter continues that theme while moving further outward from the "center". How, it asks more pointedly, has Law and Economics shaped "globalization" itself? Whereas I suggested in prior chapters that the movement is more textured and complex in ideological and political persuasion than most outsiders realize, I argue here that the global impact of this movement has been more uniformly imperious. That is to say, the influence of Law and Economics on globalization has been generally *neoliberal*: it advocates for market-based economic development, prioritizes trade liberalization, and emphasizes individual agency over structural determination of utility and welfare.

Although a deeper look at globalization is the focus of the pages below, some introductory remarks about it for purposes of definition are in order. By *globalization*, I am referring to both a process of change, and changes themselves by which the world comes to feel more interconnected, and smaller than before. There is much to unpack in this statement. Globalization is a "process" in that it has come in progressive steps rather than all at once, and these steps have been largely man-made and deliberate. Although the purpose of making the world a smaller place may not be the end goal of most stakeholders, the purposes of incremental advances in speed, convenience, and translation—for example, in international online banking—have. But globalization is also the

DOI: 10.4324/9781003350767-4

resulting change: once it becomes feasible and reasonably affordable to fly nonstop from Los Angeles to Dubai, then that capability itself becomes part of the global human condition. Moreover, one's choice to take advantage of this opportunity itself advances the interconnectedness of the world; we become participants in the process thanks to the resulting changes it has enabled. In this way, process and result work together to hasten what we call globalization.

The definition I offered above also makes use of the word "feel", as in "comes to feel more interconnected". This is purposeful as well. One could easily examine or discuss globality from the standpoint of objective indicators; many in sociology, political science, and even computer science, have done this. They look at numbers of international phone calls, the number of people "foot voting" through migration, the volume of digital information transmitted back and forth through transnational data connections, or even total sums of money wired across borders in a given period of time. But, faithful to the humanist approaches of anthropology, sociology, and cultural studies, this chapter considers the interpretive dimension of globalization foremost: how is it lived and encountered by most people, and how is it reflected in their lives? We know from a long series of studies in these humanistic fields that experiential data can come from all directions. Aiwha Ong wrote early on about a transnational elite that lives new types of lives and citizenship *between* Asian countries and the United States (Ong 1999). Hankins (2014) has taken a multi-sited approach to study the international trade in leather by literally "following the product" through the global supply chain. And Anna Tsing (2015) has connected the experiential human side of globalization with the ecological impacts by documenting and analyzing the economy of rare-mushroom collection and trading between the Pacific Northwest and Asia. These are just a few examples where we have access to rich, deep interpretive data about how the process and results of change have reconfigured lives into global networks embodied by real people in real localities. Without these accounts, one might assume globalization is just something between corporations, governments, or banks; instead, we have learned, it is also a development in human experience and consciousness.

But, in a book of this nature, this begs the question whether and how globalization can be properly studied or understood using Law and Economics. Like much that this movement did prior to the 1990s—when most scholars would date the "start" of our contemporary global condition—the "economic analysis of" law and globalization could be seen as just one of many new fields, or areas, or subdisciplines that Law and Economics has claimed for itself by leaning into adjacent subject areas. It had already achieved successes in Law and Literature and Legal History, to name a few. But extending "the economic analysis of" to global law and politics raises a new set of limitations that were perhaps not present in older extensions of its theory and methods.

Namely, the underlying premises of Law and Economics—debatable though they may be—are clearly grounded in specific times and spaces of human social history. The previous chapters have duly expressed this already, so a short recap will suffice here. Rational choice is the first of these premises. Most keenly associated with the Chicago School, it is in fact a near-universal in that even those attempting to challenge it with behavioral research are still bound by the language and primacy of rationalist models. These originate far back in time, but their earliest modern popularizer may have been Adam Smith, who famously wrote that,

It is not from the benevolence of the butcher, the brewer, or the baker, that we expect our dinner, but from their regard to their own interest. We address ourselves, not to their humanity but to their self-love, and never talk to them of our own necessities but of their advantages.

(Smith 2019)

This self-interest is nowadays referred to as rational choice—it means that individuals will go after what they consider to be in their best interest, and that anything less would be irrational. Smith's commentary refers to the fact that entire markets succeed in efficient production and distribution because of this tendency among individuals, provided those individuals act as such. Above all else, however, this model of human behavior was only possible once philosophers had reframed the definition of personhood itself as comprising "thinkers and doers", rather than as a mere follower of kings and queens. That step was part of what we now call the Western Enlightenment—a time in European history abetted by colonial expansion and new consumer habits, such as coffee-drinking, that saw a flourishing in human thought and writing about the nature of human freedom, power, and self-determination. In other words, "rational choice", ebbing and flowing as it has since the 18th century in the West, is very much a product of the Enlightenment thought revolution, and remains embedded in economic and legal ideas that stem from this period.

The value of market exchange is a second major premise. As in the case of Smith's butcher, brewer, and baker, classical and neoclassical economists have believed that the net result of individual pursuit of self-interest is a market system in which little to no outside control is needed to ensure production and distribution of social products. In his other writings, this self-regulating capacity of the market is known as the "invisible hand" (Smith 2018). The popularity of this idea has risen and fallen over the decades—its low likely came in the Keynesian wave of New Deal corrective policies—but it has, since Smith's day, always been with us. It, too, is a product of Anglo-Saxon political economic thought developed during and after the 18th century.

And of course, efficiency is still another key premise tightly situated in European intellectual history for roughly 300 years. In this case, it is mainly Jeremy Bentham whom we have to thank for the elevation of efficiency into a kind of ethical framework for decision-making and judgment. In his *Introduction to the Principles of Morals and Legislation* Bentham (2018) lays out the "principle of utility", a premise by which "all" human beings naturally tend to maximize their pleasure and minimize their pain. Faced with having to make ethical decisions in society, politics should be guided by this same principle to arrive at solutions that create the "greatest good for the greatest number". The advantages of this guiding approach, Bentham says, are several: utilitarianism allows for universalizing—it is something all living things can relate to; it allows for translation between seemingly disparate actions—a trip to a waterpark versus a trip to a cemetery are not really comparable except insofar as we can readily discern how much pleasure and pain each may bring us; and utilitarianism presumes equality—reasonable minds may disagree on what causes pleasure and pain (and in what quantities) but by considering the "aggregate" utility of everyone, we must assume that each person's feelings count equally in any given system. And yet, despite the appeals of universalizability, translatability, and equality, it is clear that utilitarianism as an economic premise *and* as an ethical framework is born of the specific place and time during and after Bentham's life. It was, in short, another product of the Western philosophical renaissance of the 18th century.

Meanwhile, the legal tradition that furnishes the institutions for lawyer-economists to study and advocate legal change is also particular. It is not a coincidence that the movement was born out of scholarship in the English common-law tradition. This form of legal system evolved in the same geographic and temporal spaces as the modern "market economy", and it shares some of its key theorists with classical economics: Locke, Smith, and Bentham among others. Indeed, these three thinkers almost single-handedly gave us, respectively, our baseline notions of private property, free markets, and utility, and all three commented on both law and economics in their work. Law and Economics, born of this tradition, is therefore substantially a product of Anglo-American common law and germinated in a period when European-style social welfare ideas were experiencing critical pushback from various quarters.

All this is to set up the following observation for discussion in this chapter: Law and Economics—born of a highly particular Western legal and political tradition—experiences substantial tension in values when it encounters the people and institutions of the world through globalization. So far, this "people and institutions of the world" has remained fairly anonymous—a faceless mass that we know is out there but know little more about it. And this—a substantial knowledge gap between the familiar and the foreign—is the basis for the kinds of cognitive bias that researchers in psychology have long identified. Human beings tend to favor themselves and their friends and family, and we tend to believe ideas and values that are long familiar to us are superior to ideas and values that are new and practiced by others. Anthropologists are perhaps most familiar with this tendency, and with efforts to try to understand it. They travel far and wide and "embed" themselves in other cultures and value systems. They start from a premise—which I oversimplify here for the moment—that the "natives are always right". Lawyer-economists, meanwhile, commenting on legal or economic practices in Eastern and Southern countries of the world, tend to do the opposite; their technical training seems to guarantee the superiority of their expertise over and above "local knowledge"—particularly in matters of resource production and allocation.

The Chicago School and International Affairs

The previous chapters already made steady reference to the role that the Chicago School played in international development during the 20th century. The most prominent example of this is usually the case of the "Chicago Boys" in Chile. Brought to the United States on fellowships for graduate study at the University of Chicago, these several dozen young men were trained in the price-theory and anti-statist approach popularized by Milton Friedman, and returned to their home country following the violent military coup of General Augusto Pinochet in 1973 (Paley 2001). Their liberalization reforms became the basis for the "Chile Miracle" in which their country made great leaps forward in economic development during the 1970s through the 1990s but did so at the expense of the welfare of the Chilean working class and indigenous populations (2001).

Another strong example occurred 20 years previously, when Friedman was invited to Paris in the fall of 1950. There, European statesmen were developing the architecture of the new European Coal and Steel Community (E.C.S.C.)—an economic union (of sorts) intended to bring France and Germany together through economic cooperation in the rebuilding of postwar Europe. Friedman, a consultant for a Marshall Plan project, formally opposed the Schuman Plan for the E.C.S.C. on the basis that it would overly involve governments in European economic life (Ebenstein 2007, 80).

A far more contemporary example of Chicago Law and Economics in international affairs comes in the work of Eric Posner, son of Richard Posner, and his co-authors on the welfarist implications of international law. For decades, scholars in international affairs have theorized and strategized the possibility of a "world government"— a U.N.-like body with palpable executive powers to enforce international law, particularly in matters of peacebuilding and human rights. As an adjunct to political science, most in international affairs have theorized this possibility (or impossibility) from the standpoint of democratic and institutional legitimacy: how would a world government exist and receive respect from world nations unless it adequately represents *all* their various constituents, and how would it do that when even national governments struggle in this respect? Elsewhere in the international business literature, Manuel Velasquez has written about the status of the moral obligation for corporations to pursue a "global common good". Such obligation, Velasquez writes, is entirely lacking under the "traditional realist" perspective originated by Thomas Hobbes, who said effectively that there can be no prevailing moral code in the absence of any effective enforcement body (Velasquez 2006, 190). Though seemingly tangential as a comment on multinational corporations, this insight is actually transferrable to the international (e.g., between states) domain. If *states* can act in large part without international enforcement oversight in most cases, how can *they* be held to pursuing the "common good" of the international community?

Writing in 2006, Posner cleverly argues that a single "world government" is plausible, but that it requires a "welfarist approach". Welfarism, we have already noted, is the approach in economics that considers the general well-being of the community as a key measure of economic policies. Above all, it takes into account whether and how much the various members of any community are having their "preferences" met. The current nation-state system, he writes, is largely a function of social groupings at the highest level that permits "economies of scale" while still fulfilling the utilitarian preferences of the maximum number. Larger political units—for example the United Nations—struggle to meet the welfare needs because their constituent group is too large and heterogeneous (Posner 2006, 490–1). The merits of the argument are best left to a larger volume; for our purposes, of greatest interest is this reimagining of the international political-legal regime in economistic terms, and not just pure economic theory but in the particular lawyer-economist form that has distilled economic thought to a version of utilitarianism.

And what of the impact of this lawyer-economist perspective on international affairs?

At 95 citations, this particular 2006 paper of Posner's is actually one of his lesser-cited works. His most-cited work, a 2005 co-authored book entitled *The Limits of International Law*, has been used in other scholarship a total of 2,500 times, with other international law articles also near the top of his highest-impact work. The point in saying this is to cap off this section with some hard evidence that the "Law and Economics of international law" has emerged as a highly productive and impactful subfield within the discipline and that it is theorized and practiced by one of the most high-profile University of Chicago scholars currently active.

From its early origins in classical economics grounded in the Western Enlightenment values of rationality, markets, and efficiency, Law and Economics emerged in the early 20th century to revive these concepts as the core of a new approach to policy that made particular sense in the United States a few decades after Keynesian ideas had already "saved" the country from the Depression. By that time, with the Cold War underway, state economic intervention came to signify diminished freedom and democracy, and the neoclassical approach growing at Chicago began to exert considerable influence. As that influence grew to include Europe and Latin America, it ran up against the discrete social and political needs of those continents impacted by war or ravaged by colonialism. The values Chicago economics represented in those days ran squarely against many of the "preferences" for social welfare and social justice present in those other contexts, and yet they managed to greatly influence the new institutions that emerged anyway. The extension of a welfarist approach by Eric Posner and others in more recent years supports a view that the influence of neoclassical economics well beyond the United States is a *fait accompli*—an established fact. But how have local cultures shifted in response? Is the spread of Anglo-Saxon economism in the 20th and 21st centuries strictly a game for academics, or has it permeated the societies of other countries as well? The short answer will be that, yes, it has permeated global culture in local contexts, and the manner by which this has occurred is frequently called "neoliberalism".

Neoliberalism and "Structural Adjustment"

In 1944, more than 700 people gathered in Bretton Woods, New Hampshire, for the United Nations Monetary and Financial Conference. This gathering, later called the Breton Woods Conference, was convened for the purpose of establishing a global, postwar financial system for the world economy. The Agreement signed by the attendees led to establishment of the International Monetary Fund (I.M.F.) and the World Bank. And at the insistence of the United States, it tied global currencies to the gold standard and the U.S. Dollar. One of the key purposes of the conference and agreement was to establish a global financial order after WWII such that losing countries would not be condemned to exorbitant debt and resulting inflation. This was based on the lesson of the Treaty of Versailles, the post-WWI convention that held Germany liable for Europe's rebuilding and led to severe economic instability. And as historians have pointed out, it was largely this instability that allowed the Nazis' rise to power democratically in the 1930s.

The United States was largely at the center of the Bretton Woods agreement. Whereas the British economist John Maynard Keynes advocated for a proposal that victor countries must invest directly in postwar debtor nations, this plan was opposed by the American delegation which instead favored establishment of the I.M.F. The International Monetary fund today is worth approximately $1.32 trillion. That sum results from member states paying in to the general fund with the understanding that debtor countries can—as a last resort—borrow from this fund. The Soviet Union opted out of signing the final accord, which further set the Allies and Soviets on diverging or conflicting paths within the world system. For smaller debtor countries, the choice for economic aid was between these two centers of power, and this made it difficult for developing countries, especially, to remain neutral under the global pressure to align with either communism or capitalism. Offering itself as a more democratic, market-based alternative to "command" economies under socialism, the Breton Woods system gave aid to war-torn and developing nations while spreading the Western, neoclassical economic ideas of private property, market exchange, and efficiency performance metrics. But what if debtor countries did not already have these institutions in place?

To ensure that countries accepting money from the I.M.F. and World Bank used the resources in ways harmonious with Western politics and economics, these international financial institutions developed the policy of "conditionality". This means that they would attach contingencies to offers of economic aid and to offers to join the Western economic system. For elites in the developing world, this posed little problem; educated in English and in the ways of Western institutions such as law and finance, the condition of "structural adjustment" meant effectively that doing business at high levels in those countries would become easier and more transparent. But for local people making a living closer to the ground—farmers, for example—structural adjustment programs such as the removal of price controls and import tariffs meant that competition with other farmers would now take place on the global stage, and that fluctuations in global market prices could bring changes in sustainability to one's own local operation. The full list of structural adjustment conditions is referred to as the "Washington Consensus" and it can include devaluation of currency, budget balancing, austerity measures, enhancement of foreign investor legal rights, anti-corruption measures, privatization, removal of price controls, increased foreign direct investments, and enhancement of domestic resource extraction. For a closer look at these in operation, some case studies may be useful.

Mexico

Mexico began receiving conditional aid from the I.M.F. and World Bank in 1982. From that year, the national government began implementing the policy adjustments classically promoted by these international institutions. Early on, therefore, it cut "non-productive" government spending; this led to a slashing of the country's healthcare budget from 4.7 to 2.7 percent of public spending (Heredia and Purcell 1994). As one study points out, this led to a tripling of the infant mortality rate in Mexico between 1980 and 1992 (1994). Meanwhile, the adjustment toward liberalization in trade policies had the effect of forcing small and medium-sized agricultural producers to compete with global imports, and of creating a borrowing crisis as domestic interest rates were raised to prevent capital from leaving the country. This pressure, it has been said, affected some 80 percent of the country's workforce. And finally, due in part to privatization and deregulation imposed by the I.M.F. and the World Bank, income inequality grew considerably during the 1980s. Whereas the top 20 percent of earners commanded 48 percent of national income in 1984, this number had risen to 54 percent by 1992 (1994). Among the beneficiaries was Carlos Slim Helu, C.E.O. of Telmex, the nation's largest telecommunications firm, who to this day remains Mexico's richest person at $78 billion of net worth in a country whose per capita G.D.P. in 2021 was roughly $10,000 (Brown 2022; World Bank 2023).

Among the key victims of structural adjustment in Mexico have been the farmers of Chihuahua. Bordering on the U.S. state of Texas to the north, Chihuahua was home to a thriving corn- and bean-farming industry until about 1992. In 1988, Mexico received a World Bank loan aimed at reducing international food subsidies, minimizing government controls and subsidies, and liberalizing agricultural exports. The results, as may be expected, were to stifle credit to small farmers and subject local produce to global prices, leading in turn to growth in export production and a surge in cheap imported grains. For local peasants, the impact was disastrous, and it sent many scrambling to find seasonal work north of the border in the United States. Said one Chihuahuan farmer,

My husband is always here during planting season, but the rest of the year he spends working in the United States. He and four children in Texas, Florida, Colorado and New Mexico take care of all the family expenses and they take turns helping with the planting. When we are short of money, my husband and my children are contracted to work in the apple orchards or to do some other work in the countryside.

(quoted in Heredia and Purcell 1994)

While these economic effects in Mexico have been starkly felt, and indeed led ultimately to the rural uprising in the southern state of Chiapas in 1994 which became a symbol for the worldwide anti-globalization movement (see Gilman-Opalsky 2008), Mexico still incurred less institutional pressure to Westernize its legal system than the economic giant China.

China

The case study of China offers a slightly different picture of the law and economics of globalization as it unfolded in the developing world. China today is the world's second most-populous country, with roughly 1.4 billion people as of this writing—despite decades of population-growth control policies. The country was ruled as a dynastic empire from the third century B.C. up until the early 20th century, whereupon various political reform factions rose up against the emperor and established the First Republic of China. Importantly, the agitation and revolution leading to the end of imperial rule resulted in part from the humiliations of European colonialism, including the Opium Wars of the 19th century. In the power vacuum of the post-imperial period, a civil war broke out between rival factions vying for control and planning of Chinese modernization. From 1927 until 1949, with an eight-year hiatus during World War II, the rival nationalist and communist parties fought until the latter Chinese Communist Party (C.C.P.) emerged victorious in October 1949. Chairman of the party was Mao Zedong, who became the first premier of the new People's Republic of China.

The People's Republic was founded on Marxist-Leninist principles. Initially a nationalist in his younger years, Mao became familiar with Marxism while working as a librarian at Peking University and helped to establish the first communist party and the Workers' and Peasants' Red Army. Mao instituted several historic communist reforms in China that continue to influence the country's politics, culture and economy. One was a Land Reform campaign that confiscated farmland from owners, saw those owners executed by the thousands, and then redistributed land holdings to peasants in small allotments. In 1958, Mao instituted the "Great Leap Forward" which aimed to convert the agricultural economy of China into a modern communist economy based upon farmworker communes in the countryside. This five-year-plan set such ambitious goals for farm production that local bosses took substantial grain produce from peasants to meet exorbitant quotas in order to appear productive, while leaving local families with almost nothing. This caused one of the worst famines in human history resulting in between 15 and 55 million deaths due to starvation. Finally, in the last ten years of his life, Mao oversaw the "Cultural Revolution" which sought to restore revolutionary fervor by encouraging youth groups to rise up against any remaining dissent in the country, which in turn led to another purge totaling up to one million deaths.

The legal culture of China coming out of the Mao period from 1949 to 1976 was a combination of traditional Confucian legal philosophy and the modern communist view of law as an extension of party ideology. On the traditional side, it consisted of Confucian concepts such as *li* and *fa*; the former translating to "ritual", whereas the latter more properly means formal "law" (Peerenboom 1998). These two concepts reveal much about the way the Chinese legal order operated in the era prior to modern globalization. Whereas *fa* corresponds to the institutionalized, codified, written law backed by the coercive power of the State, *li* describes the domain of social norms and customs that govern people's behavior not through the threat of state violence or coercion but by the prospect of social, isolation, and disavowal. For the legal anthropologists and comparative lawyers who study this, the coexistence of these two forms of social control is a textbook example of legal pluralism at work on a massive scale. As some studies have suggested, it leads to many cases in which formal "law" must be violated in order to comply with social custom—an often-higher priority in Chinese legal culture. Along with this bifurcation of the legal universe, there is also the coexistence of Confucian law with modern communist legal doctrine. Here, concepts such as private property ownership and individual employment contracts are treated differently than they would be in Western legal culture. The entire purpose of communist law, many have said, is to support the ideological platform on which communist parties are founded. So, minimal protections for private ownership and minimal protection for private employers become the norm—especially after Mao's "Cultural Revolution"—and maximal protections for the legal position of the Party and its leadership get priority.

One of the key implications of these legal ideas was a general unfriendliness toward foreign participation in China's economic development. Western countries wishing to do business in China would encounter numerous obstacles entering its market and establishing legal protections once there (Glenza 2014). Two examples are illustrative. The first involves Chinese intellectual property law. Many western companies, well before actively entering the Chinese market, were already confronted with the problem that their products were being illegally copied, imitated, and sold there. As the Chinese economy began to liberalize in the 1990s, the emergence of a Chinese middle class drove a demand for European and American goods as luxury items indicative of value and success. Not only that, but around the world the demand for cheap knockoff products grew, thanks to increased tourism, currency exchange strengths, and cultural globalization (e.g., more and more non-Westerners exposed to European and American consumer culture). Western companies, in theory, lost millions of dollars in market value thanks to the influx of imitation goods, and they began to lobby their home governments to do something about this. One result was the creation, for the first time, of Chinese intellectual property laws designed to protect domestic and foreign manufacturers and retailers from copycats.

Another example was, until the 2000s, the relative absence of foreign companies directly investing in the Chinese economy. In 1993, following two decades of economic reforms slowly opening to the West, China passed the Corporation Law limiting the degree of ownership by the State in private companies. In the 2000s, China sought admission to the World Trade Organization and, as such, adopted a series of accelerated trade liberalization policies. Between 2001 and 2004 state-owned enterprises decreased by 48 percent (Brandt et al. 2010). And by the mid-2000s, private companies all over the world were vying for entry into the Chinese market, viewing its population of 1 billion people as an "untapped" captive audience for products such as soft drinks, apparel, electronics, and motor vehicles. But the problem of legal culture still remained. For China to gain full admission to the W.T.O., it would need more than just economic liberalization. As the W.T.O. itself demanded, China would need to adopt widespread legal reforms crafting its legal system in the image of the West's.

The World Trade Organization is an intergovernmental organization dedicated to the regulation of international trade. It was founded in 1995 as a successor to the General Agreement on Tariffs and Trade (G.A.T.T.) treaty that has been in place since 1948. China achieved "observer" status to G.A.T.T. in 1986 and sought to become a founding member of W.T.O. before being denied this status by the United States, Japan, and other countries. The main objection to Chinese membership had been its reliance on economic central planning and lack of transparency and open competition. It had operated as a Soviet-style socialist planned economy with minimal participation in the world economy from the 1940s until the late 1970s, following a decade of warming diplomatic relations with the United States (Farah and Cima 2009).

Between 1986 and 2001, as a condition for joining the W.T.O., China was asked to engage in a series of structural reforms to ensure fair competition and property rights within its borders. One of these was a commitment to remove customs barriers, thereby opening China to trade from other W.T.O. member states (Farah and Cima 2009). This included a condition to reduce direct subsidies to domestic producers, which China had utilized for decades. A second major condition was the requirement of a new intellectual property rights regime. Intellectual property, as an institution, emerged in the West alongside modern printing techniques and artistic mechanical reproduction. In China, no such concept had ever existed, let alone been protected in law. In 1984, China adopted its first-ever patent law legislation, and in 1994 it signed the Trade-Related Aspects of Intellectual Property Rights (TRIPs) agreement setting minimum protections required of all W.T.O. member states.

But the installation of new, Western-inspired property rights by itself would prove ineffective under existing Confucian and Communist legal institutions. Farah and Cima point out two general tracks for Chinese intellectual property (IP) disputes: administrative and judicial (2009, 107). The administrative cases for both patent and trademark disputes roughly doubled in the years following adoption and implementation of TRIPs. But, on the judicial side, this level of growth was met with a new problem. Chinese courts, as well as the country's legal profession, were ill-prepared to grow with the spreading "rule of law"—particularly in rural areas.

Thus, the Chinese government in response planned a major expansion and Westernization of the nation's legal education and legal profession. Legal anthropologist Matthew Erie offers an incisive case study of Chinese legal education during this period. In the mid-2000s, he conducted long-term fieldwork at Tsinghua University School of Law—an institution already modeled on the structure of Yale Law School. Erie documented the rise of a new legal degree offering in China, the J.M. or *juris master* meant to parallel the American *juris doctor* degree (albeit correcting the odd nomenclature of "doctorate" since U.S. and international law schools offer the "master of legal letters" or LL.M as an "advanced" law degree post-J.D.). Whereas legal training in the traditional Chinese law schools was a highly academic and abstract affair (not unlike European legal education), the new J.M. was meant to emphasize "practice" and "critical thinking" skills like American law schools are known to do (Erie 2009, 61):

The JM degree has been interpreted widely by Chinese academics as essential to the modernization of China's legal system and as a requirement to building ROL [rule of law]. Scholars have viewed it as vital to realizing former President Jiang Zemin's *yifazhiguo* "rule the county according to law" and preparing lawyers to compete for legal services in post-accession WTO China. The overriding purpose of the JM is to produce better legal practitioners.

(Erie 2009, 68)

With the offering of this new degree and its replacement of the primary legal credential, the Chinese Ministry of Justice also ordered the training of hundreds of thousands of new lawyers to fill judicial and advocate roles in the new economy. In 2013, there was a total of 250,000 licensed lawyers in the country, whereas this number was projected to reach 620,000 by 2022 (Chen 2020). To get there, hundreds of new law schools were opened across the country. In the 1990s, there were fewer than 200 law schools; today, there are approximately 650 (Wang et. al. 2017, 257; Li 2019, 554).

Lest we lose track amid all these numbers and all this growth, the above sections have surveyed cases in the history of economic globalization with attention to some of the legal implications such changes have brought. In Mexico, where trade liberalization imposed by the I.M.F. and World Bank created local crises in production and employment, the indirect effect of economic reforms was to create a problem for legal immigration policy in the United States. With Mexican farmers decreasingly able to support their families in the new competitive world economy, it was inevitable that more workers would seek opportunity—even if seasonally—in the powerful neighbor country to the north. In China, similar liberalization conditions imposed by the W.T.O. were meant to open the Chinese population as a market for global goods and services, but they secondarily required major reforms in the legal order of China ramifying all the way down to the basic structure and geographic distribution of legal education in the country.

It is fitting that many of the problems caused by economic globalization warranted legal solutions. It could be said that these problems result from high-level policies and institutions developed in the image of Chicago School economics and first "tested" in the 1970s in countries such as Chile. The doctrine of economic "shocks" to bring developing nations into the global economy was a direct descendant of ideas first developed by the group of price-theory economists gathered largely around the law school at the University of Chicago in the mid-20th century.

Figure 3.1 Widely viewed sign from the 1999 "Battle of Seattle" protests against the W.T.O.

Photo credit: "WTO protest sign (14988892087)" by geraldford from Seattle, U.S.A., is licensed under CC BY-SA 2.0.

A Global Legal-Economic Order?

The Mexico and China cases of legal and economic globalization illustrate a few common themes. First and foremost is the emergence of a new global legal-economic order in which the restructuring of norms and the restructuring of exchange are seen as two sides of the same coin. In these contexts, human and civil rights do matter, but they are in fact subsidiary to the larger priority of stabilizing and opening up markets. Second, is the institution-building function of legal-economic "planners"—experts from either or both law and economics who are granted outsized influence over global economic policy and practice. And finally, third, is the understanding or assumption that economics lie at the root of empires, decolonization, and development.

These connections between global economic change and refined legal expertise are just a few examples of a larger nexus observed even more widely by recent scholars of "law and capitalism". The comparative law scholar Annelise Riles has written that lawyers became the engineers of a new global financial system in which transactions across vast distances were made instantaneously by the legal technology of "collateral" (2011). By creating and refining securitized agreements, lawyers were able to allow money to move more quickly, and in higher volumes, than at any previous time in human history. Lawyers and legal expertise, in other words, sat at the core of the new global financial capitalism. More recently, Katarina Pistor has expanded this line of reasoning to suggest all of capitalism itself was made possible by legal technologies that ascribed exclusivity and value to naturally occurring resources such as land, labor, water, and minerals (2019). This then permitted business interests to trade in these resources, as well as to use them to secure other types of agreements in the early days of capitalist exchange. Without this "encoding" of raw materials as capital, the economic system we now take for granted would not have evolved over the past 600 years. Finally, Carruthers and Haliday have made similar observations about the development of a global bankruptcy law regime on the part of the large international financial institutions such as the World Bank, arguing that law now sits at the heart of the new networked global financial order (2007). Each of these observations—though not explicitly tied to the story of Law and Economics—expands this discussion to consider the role of law as such in the economic order of its surrounding context.

The historic precedent for these uses of law in a global context long predates the era of modern globalization. Recall from Chapter 1 of this book that in 1947 Frederick Hayek organized a workshop at Mont Pelerin in the Swiss Alps. There, with funding from the Volker Fund, Hayek was able to assemble roughly 40 international scholars from the United States and Europe for a ten-day conference on free-market principles and policy opportunities. There, the purpose was not to simply initiate a discussion to be continued separately in participant home countries; it was to consolidate the role of a small group of libertarian academics and writers. Four guests are significant for this discussion; Hayek had invited Aaron Director and Frank Knight—both faculty at the University of Chicago and key to the economization of the law school (see Chapters 1 and 2, this volume), as well as their students Milton Friedman and George Stigler (Kolasky 2020). Henry Simons, who was mentioned by Hayek in his opening address, likely would have been in attendance but for his death and replacement by Director at Chicago the year prior. The attendees met twice a day for the duration of the conference to discuss topics from "'Free' Enterprise or Competitive Order", "Full Employment and Monetary Reform", and "Wage Policy and Trade Unions", among other things. By far one of the biggest running concerns throughout the meeting was the specter of "collectivism" in Europe and North America in the wake of the Depression and World War II:

> In his opening statement on the first panel, Director began by warning that the "collectivist" claim that the greater efficiency of large-scale

business enterprises made private monopolies inevitable was contributing to a trend toward greater government control of the economy and a suppression of individual freedom in both the United States and Europe. He suggested, therefore, that the panel should focus on how to alter the legal framework in order to design a more effective "competitive order".

(Kolasky 2020)

This recognition on the part of one of the earliest Law and Economics institution-builders is even more telling in hindsight. Hayek, with his Chicago School colleagues, viewed law instrumentally in global context as a means for shoring up "free market" competition against the statist political culture of postwar Keynesianism. As Kolasky (2020) has said, the meeting at Mont Pelerin is now viewed by many as the birthplace of global "neoliberalism".

But this story of global applied Law and Economics told as the origin and ultimate rise of Euro-American neoliberalism—from Mont Pelerin to the World Trade Organization—is incomplete without acknowledgment of world events in the decades between these "moments". Between 1947 and 1995, American and European countries saw their overseas colonial holdings diminish significantly. Make no mistake, however, this did not occur due to new, enlightened understandings about racial difference, political self-determination, or human freedom. Such understandings had already been circulating widely since the 18th century and yet they had not discouraged European and North American powers from seizing control of land, labor, and resources in the Eastern and Southern Hemispheres.

Decolonization

The period between World War II and the 1980s, sometimes referred to as the "Age of Decolonization", was marked by numerous bloody wars fought by local men and women to gain independence and the right to self-government. On another level, they were intended to expel American and European settlers, administrators, and military personnel from territories that had been seized from native peoples and held by force. Examples of such holdings include French control over North Africa in what is now Morocco, Algeria, Tunisia, British control over modern-day India, Pakistan, Bangladesh and Sri Lanka, as well as American control over the Philippines. White-minority colonial control in these regions was, even in the best of times, precarious. It made use of metropolitan (e.g., French-born) administrators, jurists, military officers, and so forth who represented the colonizer in the overseas territories. Many of these people moved entire families to the colonies where, ostensibly, they were promised privileged status, cheap and thus luxurious living conditions, and all the economic and legal protections they would have experienced in the home country. But similarly, colonial administrations learned that in order to maintain power and stability they would also need to develop a class of loyal, Western-educated locals to act as middlemen on the ground. Partly for this reason, colonial education of local youth was tightly controlled by settler countries (Ọlọruntimẹhin 1974). Educated in the administrative language, be it French, English, Spanish, etc., the new local elite could serve the functions of the home country in maintaining authority in a local context, all while aspiring to attaining the social and economic capital possessed by white settlers. Before earning their independence, most European colonies operated on this type of model for decades, if not centuries. Indeed, when revolutionary movements gained popularity in the mid-20th century, they were not usually led by locally educated administrative elites, because those individuals and their families had much to lose from colonial expulsion. Rather, as in the case of Ho Chi Minh in the Vietnamese independence struggle, or founders of the Indian pro-independence Ghadar Party, they were often educated abroad in places where the promise of Western liberalism had not been tempered or diluted to justify acceptance of colonial subjugation.

Law, in particular, served an important role in the colonization process. On one hand, colonial administrators needed to supplant local indigenous, Islamic, Confucian, and Hindu legal "institutions" with European ones. Without this step, concepts such as "private property ownership" or "liability for fault" would not be transferrable to colonial territories and their settlers. But on the other hand, it was often necessary to maintain a modicum of "local law" in order to prevent total breakdown in authority and social cohesion. Most of the colonial powers thus developed versions of *legal pluralism*, the idea that one "layer" of law—British common law, for example—could coexist and overlay a different layer of local or folk legal tradition and authority. The rise of the British Privy Council offers a telling example of this legal pluralism at work. In many cases involving disputes over family law, for instance, native legal authorities such as tribal elders or *qadi* (in Islamic courts) were generally entrusted to render decisions in conformity with local custom. But in cases where such decisions could not quell a dispute, or where the local institution was thought insoluble with Western ideals, local decisions could be appealed to the King's Privy Council. In hearing disputes from the colonies, the Privy Council had as its responsibility a duty to be briefed on and consider local legal culture. The Privy Council thus served as the de facto "court of last resort" for disputes arising out of the British Colonies even under Hindu, Confucian, Islamic, or other local legal norm systems.

Though some of these features transcended local context, the experience of each former colony was unique. Morocco and Tunisia gained independence from France in 1956; initially both were reestablished as monarchies, but Tunisia abolished its monarchic succession a year later and remains a republic. Algeria, lacking a clear path of monarchic succession, and more deeply intertwined with French-born and locally born ethnic French settlers, suffered a seven-year bloody war for independence before achieving autonomous statehood in 1962. Experts estimate roughly 1 to 1.5 million Algerian deaths resulted from this conflict. In India, which gained independence from England in 1947, there had been no all-out military conflict but rather a nationwide campaign of nonviolent passive resistance. Nevertheless, the number of casualties caused by England's grip on South Asia was massive. According to one scholarly estimate, between the 1880s and 1920s alone, Britain was responsible for 40 million deaths in their South Asian colony (Sullivan and Hickel 2023). For the Philippines, U.S. control was surrendered voluntarily at the conclusion of World War II per the previously established Tydings-McDuffie Act of 1934. But in addition to establishing mandatory provisions in the future Filipino Constitution and requiring the new document to be first approved by the U.S. President, it also reclassified Filipinos at home and in the United States as "aliens" and made them subject to immigration limits.

In all three cases, North African, South Asian, and Filipino former colonies were all heavily marked by the legal system of their colonizers. In present-day Algeria, for example, courts apply a version of French civil law interspersed with aspects of Islamic and Berber law in private matters. In South Asia—not to mention much of the former British "New" Commonwealth—courts apply British common law and style themselves in the black robes and white wigs of their imperial colonizers. And in the Philippines, which had been a Spanish colony far longer than an American one, the legal system consists of Roman civil law, English common law, and Islamic legal institutions and ideas. The significance of Western law to economic matters in these countries cannot be overstated. Without the Euro-American legal traditions maintaining their presence in these countries, ideas such as private property and freedom of contract might not have emerged or remained on their own. The "transplanting" of legal ideas, culture, and institutions in these places lead to more than just an interesting legal history. It set the stage for the insertion of these (and other similar) countries into the global market that became the later object of I.M.F., World Bank, and W.T.O. enforcement. In this regard, they are also held out as examples of law's role in economic development, and as proof of the righteousness of "conditionality" requirements such as Western-style rule of law in debtor nations. The resulting world order, in which national economies are now networked through liberal policies elevating trade as the primary basis for global intercourse, and in which law forms the structure on which that order is based, was described by the writers Michael Hardt and Antonio

Negri in the early 2000s as a new form of "Empire" (2000). But unlike the political "empires" of the colonial age, the new one has been largely economic in nature, and legalistic in structure.

Conclusion

The development of European empires and colonial rule long predates the modern Law and Economics movement. And yet it illustrates sharply an applied wisdom that began to take shape in the era of the classical economists and moral philosophers from Smith to Bentham. This wisdom is that economic conditions must be reinforced by legal institutions, and conversely that most legal policies come with economic consequences. In the home nations of Europe, these conditions and institutions evolved in parallel; thus it is sometimes difficult to observe the influence they had on one another. But in the colonies—everywhere from the early United States to latter-day India, for example—the law of England (or in North Africa, the law of France) had to be deliberately transplanted and installed in the new territories. This process of transplantation made use of metropolitan legal expertise, texts, and formal institutions, but it also employed cadres of native elites educated in English, French, and so forth to help administer the foreign legal bureaucracy in the new lands. To this day, the legal profession in postcolonial states remains a highly revered field for study and work, and a way for upper-class families to ensure their social status remains high from one generation to the next.

The effects of Law and Economics on contemporary globalization, I have suggested in this chapter, were greatly influenced by this history of colonial legal transplantation and administration. If we start from the present and work backwards, this lineage is clear. Today, large countries of the Global South and East employ legal systems that bear the clear marks of American, English, and European influence. In the case of India, these traces originate far back in time to the days when white British jurists oversaw common law courts in the country. In the case of China, these traces are new in origin, dating to the emergence of China as an economic superpower and its campaign to join the World Trade Organization in the 1990s. In these two cases, alone, we see approaches to Law and Economics today greatly influenced by the extant views popularized by key thinkers described in earlier chapters of this book. On their path to "accession" to the global economic treaties and trade agreements, both India and China (along with many others such as Mexico) were required to reduce state economic interventions such as farm subsidies and promote the influx of international goods and service by reducing customs, and they were audited for transparency and consistency in their legal systems.

Much of this book has emphasized the multi-textured character of Law and Economics in the United States. While it was largely associated with the "Conservative Legal Movement" and assumes the validity of neoclassical ideas about human behavior, it has also seen its share of critical writers questioning those ideas, and questioning the ideological connections to conservative politics in the United States. But, zooming out to the world stage, we can see that the Law and Economics concepts that made their way to the "rest of the world" were not so diverse. There, even under the watch of apparently liberal or progressive Western regimes, European and American statesmen—faithful to the new order of international financial institutions—endorsed a simplified neoclassical approach to supporting underdeveloped countries. This approach, as already described, views less economic oversight and control as prerequisite to developmental progress around the world. It does this by aligning market access and participation with human freedom and flourishing. And it does *that* by taking the West—most significantly America—as the paradigm example where individualism, decentralized authority, and unlimited growth seem instrumental in one of the world's major economic success stories.

But, to sociolegal scholars more attuned to issues of culture, society, and power, this application of an "American-style" relationship between economics and law raises numerous questions. Two of those stand out most here. Firstly, is it *ethical* for one part of the world to dictate the appropriate legal conditions for economic support to the rest of the world—especially when *need* for assistance is sometimes "life or death" on massive scales? Or, in the language of legal ethics, is it a form of existential *duress* to force debtor countries into vast restructuring just so that they can survive? Secondly, even if it were ethical, what are the cultural and social consequences of imposing such changes from without? Already, as documented by the French anthropologist Claude Levi-Strauss at mid-century, native cultures of the world were disappearing due to colonial contact and expansion (1976). The death toll caused by infectious diseases brought by Europeans to the New World and Global South was, by itself already devastating. Then the loss of cultural integrity in those regions due to the invasion and spread of Western languages and cultural objects greatly altered what remained of indigenous ethnic forms—albeit with resistance and pride movements emergent along the way. Now, joining those prior waves of destruction, comes the era of conditionality—prerequisites for economic global participation.

We were once concerned about fading languages and lost cultures. Today we might be more concerned about widespread narrowing of the very meanings of "justice". Human societies have long approached this idea differently, and the relative separation of cultures allowed each form of "justice" to evolve and solve problems differently—in ways uniquely suited to local contexts and ecological constraints. Today, as legal systems and institutions—not to mention theories and practices—are forced to harmonize, some of the diversity in human ingenuity on matters of justice is inevitably lost to time. In a world dominated by Western-style production, distribution, and consumption, this homogenization may seem fitting, or even "efficient". But as the human environment experiences shifts such as climate change, extreme weather, overpopulation, or global pandemics, our repertoire of solutions culled from the vast array of cultural adaptations may be significantly more limited.

References

Bentham, Jeremy. 2018. *An Introduction to the Principles of Morals and Legislation*. Farmington Hills, MI: Gale ECCO.

Brandt, Loren, Thomas G. Rawski, and John Sutton. 2008. "China's Industrial Development." In Loren Brandt, and Thomas G. Rawski eds. *China's Great Transformation*. Cambridge: Cambridge University Press, 569–632.

Brown, Lisa. 2022. "Wealthiest People in Mexico (December 5, 2022)." *CEOWorld Magazine*, December 6, https://ceoworld.biz/2022/12/06/wealthiest-people-in-mexico-december-5-2022/, Accessed May 5, 2023.

Chen, Yanru. 2020. "Rocketing up: Chinese Lawyers Increasing 148% in Ten Years." *China Justice*, https://www.chinajusticeobserver.com/a/rocketing-up-chinese-lawyers-increasing-148-percent-in-tenyears#:~:text=Yes%2C%20there%20there%20were%20more,by%20the%20end%20of%202019.&text=in%20Ten%20Years,By%20the%20end%20of%202019%2C%20there%20were%20more%20than%20473,profession%20has%20maintained%20rapid%20growth. Accessed May 15, 2023.

Haliday, Terence A., and Bruce G. Carruthers. 2007. "The Recursivity of Law: Global Norm Making and National Lawmaking in the Globalization of Corporate Insolvency Regimes." *American Journal of Sociology* 112 (4): 1135–1202.

Heredia, Carlos, and Mary Purcell. 1994. "Structural Adjustment in Mexico A Grassroots Perspective." *Structural Adjustment in Mexico A Grassroots Perspective*, Development GAP and Equipo PUEBLO. https://thedocs.worldbank.org/en/doc/381651612199543212-0240021993/original/WorldBankGroupArchivesFolder1784655.pdf. Accessed May 15, 2023.

Ebenstein, Lanny. 2007. *Milton Friedman: A Biography*. New York: St. Martin's Griffin.

Erie, Matthew. 2009. "Legal Education Reform in China Through U.S.-Inspired Transplants." *Journal of Legal Education* 59 (1): 60–96.

Farah, Paolo Davide, and Elena Cima. 2009. "China's Participation in the World Trade Organization: Trade in Goods, Services, Intellectual Property Rights and Transparency Issues." In Aurelio Lopez-Tarruella Martinez ed. *El Comercio Con China: Oportunidades Empresariales, Incertidumbres Juridicas*. Valencia, Spain: Editorial Tirant le Blanch, 83–121.

Gilman-Opalsky, Richard. 2008. *Unbounded Publics: Transgressive Public Spheres, Zapatismo, and Political Theory*. Lanham, MA: Lexington Books.

Glenza, Jessica. 2014. "Avon Pleads Guilty to Violating Foreign Corrupt Practices Act in China." *The Guardian*, December 18. https://www.theguardian.com/us-news/2014/dec/18/avon-pleads-guilty-violation-foreign-corrupt-practices-act-china.

Hankins, Joseph D. 2014. *Working Skin: Making Leather, Making a Multicultural Japan.* Berkeley, CA: University of California.

Hardt, Michael, and Antonio Negri. 2000. *Empire.* Cambridge, MA: Harvard University Press.

Kolasky, William. 2020. "Aaron Director and the Origins of the Chicago School of Antitrust Part II—Aaron Director: The Socrates of Hyde Park." *Antitrust* 35 (1) (Fall): 101–106.

Levi-Strauss, Claude. 1976. "Race and History." In Monique Layton trans. *Structural Anthropology Vol. II.* Chicago, IL: University of Chicago Press.

Li, Ruohan. 2019. "Rethinking on China's Higher Legal Education Reform." *International Journal of Information and Education Technology* 9 (8): 553–558.

Ong, Aiwha. 1999. *Flexible Citizenship: The Cultural Logics of Transnationality.* Durham, NC: Duke University.

Ọlọruntimẹhin, Olatunji. 1974. "Education for Colonial Dominance in French West Africa from 1900 to the Second World War." *Journal of the Historical Society of Nigeria* 7(2): 347–356.

Paley, Julia. 2001. *Marketing Democracy: Power and Social Movements in Post-Dictatorship Chile.* Berkeley, CA: University of California.

Peerenboom, Randall. 1998. "Law and Ritual in Chinese Philosophy." In Edward Craig ed. *The Routledge Encyclopedia of Philosophy.* New York: Routledge, 442–454.

Pistor, Katarina. 2019. *The Code of Capital: How the Law Creates Wealth and Inequality.* Princeton, NJ: Princeton University Press.

Posner, Eric. 2006. "International Law: A Welfarist Approach." *University of Chicago Law Review* 73(2): 487–544.

Brandt, Loren, Thomas G. Rawski, and John Sutton. 2008. "China's Industrial Development." In Loren Brandt, and Thomas G. Rawski eds. *China's Great Transformation.* Cambridge: Cambridge University Press, 569–632.

Riles, Annelise. 2011. *Collateral Knowledge: Legal Reasoning in the Global Financial Markets.* Chicago, IL: University of Chicago Press.

Smith, Adam. 2019. *The Wealth of Nations.* Mineola, NY: Ixia Press.

Sullivan, Dylan, and Jason Hickel. 2023. "Capitalism and Extreme Poverty: A Global Analysis of Real Wages, Human Height, and Mortality Since the Long 16th Century." *World Development* 161: 1–18.

Tsing, Anna L. 2015. *The Mushroom at the End of the World: On the Possibility of Life in Capitalist Ruins.* Princeton, NJ: Princeton University.

Velasquez, Manuel. 2017. "International Business, Morality, and the Common Good." In Fritz Allhoff, Alexander Sager, and Anand Vaidya eds. *Business in Ethical Focus: An Anthology,* 2nd ed. Petersborough, ON: Broadview Press, 187–197.

Wang, Zhihou, Sida Liu, and Xueyao Li. 2017. "Internationalizing Chinese Legal Education in the Early Twenty-First Century." *Journal of Legal Education* 66 (2): 237–266.

World Bank. 2023. "Mexico Overview", https://ceoworld.biz/2022/12/06/wealthiest-people-in-mexico-december-5-2022/, Accessed May 5, 2023.

Conclusion
Toward a "Critical" Law and Economics

Introduction

Contrary to what some believe, the study of law and the study of economics by themselves are not naturally ideological in any political sense. Law and legal scholarship have been mobilized throughout history to serve liberal and conservative causes; and while they *can* be used to protect the interests of the rich and powerful against the less-endowed masses, they have clearly also been used to challenge those interests. Similarly, economics by itself is not a conservative discipline or discourse. It examines all things related to production, exchange, distribution, and consumption, but it can take either positive (e.g., descriptive) or normative forms and, depending on the conditions in place at any given moment, can support either change *or* stasis in those. Both Marx and Weber were trained as lawyers, and both wrote extensively on economics, but neither could be considered "conservative".

Despite the fact that American-style Law and Economics has been generally associated, by outsiders, with being a brand of "conservative legal movement", this appellation captures only part of its emergence and success. And to be sure, given the very material demands of academic scholarship and community-building, the harmony between libertarian-style Law and Economics and large American business interests was instrumental in procuring the resources badly needed to make this movement a success. And yet, the American legal professoriate is by no means a "conservative" block. As the dozens of interviews I have conducted reveal, most lawyer-economists consider themselves and their colleagues to be "left-of-center" on most political issues today. This often means that, faced with some of the libertarian excesses of their subfield from the past, for example, the ethical imperative of "wealth maximization", many lawyer-economists today are able to disavow these as precisely long since "past". All of this may seem like a call for research subtlety and detailed qualitative data collection, but it is more than that.

DOI: 10.4324/9781003350767-5

In this concluding chapter, I want to suggest that Law and Economics tells us something new and interesting about *neoliberalism*, because the former functions as a microcosm for the knowledge economy that created and sustains the latter. This is something quite different than saying Law and Economics has merely served neoliberalism as one of its sharpest tools. There are, instead, common elements in both that have led to their mutual synergy. In other words, the success of Law and Economics and the success of neoliberalism—including their collections of large, seemingly objective data on which their policy proposals are based, are rooted in a common feature: the capacity to appeal to *both* conservative and progressive worldviews, to recruit and absorb thought and policy leaders from different sides, and to appear "objective", that is to say, non-ideological, most of the time.

This is not to say that thinkers on the far Right and Left of the political spectrum are found in large numbers supporting either Law and Economics or neoliberalism. It is to suggest, rather, that the "middle" position occupied by most people by definition, is uniquely susceptible to the kinds of "objectivism" both positions embrace strongly. In a world of "alternative facts" and "post-truth", this susceptibility is somewhat understandable; but it is very noteworthy that the power relations and epistemologies that allow creation of "data" often themselves shape the latter in ways that reinforce the worldview of those collecting and analyzing it.

Additionally, both Law and Economics and neoliberalism share a relatively strong suspicion about "the State" and its ability to serve public welfare. At one extreme are those who repeat the libertarian mantra that—when it comes to regulating social and economic behavior— "the market knows best". At another are those who see potential in government incentives to make the world more livable but also deep flaws in policies and their enforcement around matters such as taxes and expenditures. As flagged in the introduction, few writers on this topic are as generally relevant or as telling as Michel Foucault. In his final decade, Foucault gave a series of lectures at the Collège de France which seemed to reach out to Chicago economics for inspiration about the intellectual course of human freedom. Foucault, a onetime communist and intellectual activist in France through the tumultuous 1960s, grew disillusioned in the 1970s with party politics and liberation ideologies that had seemed to go nowhere. In Chicago economists such as Gary Becker, Foucault saw in the shift of focus to individualized emancipation through market citizenship a new opportunity for human liberation in the purest sense. Conceivably, Foucault's own non-conventional personal life—subject to the scrutiny and judgment of the French academic elite—inspired his partial embrace of American-style libertarian views on human freedom. In this regard, we might say *his* approach grew more "methodologically individualist" as he approached the 1980s. Unfortunately, the new decade saw the neoliberal position instrumentalized by demagogues in the West to undermine union solidarity, the welfare state, and accepted approaches to public finance. This move was one from "economics as freedom" to "economics as efficiency"—the former a humanistic approach, the latter a scientific one. In this transformation, the chief casualty seems to have been deep *ethical* reflection, whereas the chief beneficiary appears to have been cost–benefit thinking

Efficiency Revisited

Cost–benefit analysis has become a predominant standard by which justice is measured in Law and Economics. One reason is that the legal system uses compensation as a key remedy in property, contract, and accident law cases. Historically, under Western canons of corrective justice, a wrongdoer who violates a property right, breaks an agreement, or causes accidental harm has created a moral imbalance that must be corrected. This correction has usually been compelled legally in the form of monetary damages. When such damages have functioned as a kind of punishment, they help to impose "liability" on the wrongdoer. When such damages have functioned as simply a tax or a toll—a mere gatekeeper—on conducting a harmful behavior, they are considered to impose a "property right" that must be acquired by the wrongdoer after the fact (see Calabresi and Melamed 1972)

The widespread adoption of efficiency in law generally, thanks to Law and Economics, has had sweeping implications for distributive justice. The expectation that economic winners should be able to compensate losers in situations when new rules benefit the former is largely hypothetical. There has been, in fact, little effort to ensure winners actually do compensate losers over time. Given this fact, efficiency arguments have seemingly benefited those who could, largely on paper, compensate others even if they never do it (Liscow 2018).

Returning to the topic of human organs in a society that needs them, why do we not then allow a market as an efficient means to distribute organs? Perhaps it is because under a new law allowing organ sales, the wealthy would simply pay a lot to be first in line for a new organ and the poor would be outbid and either left empty-handed or with organs no one else wanted. Under modern efficiency theory, the wealthy would just have to compensate the poor for this unfortunate imbalance. And yet we still don't allow this. This is because the very idea of a market in human body parts—not to mention the perverse incentives it would create in the world, especially among the poor—is not palatable to most citizens. It would simply mimic the prevailing distribution of wealth in society. And the moral burden this would cause most of us is too much to allow even an "efficient" market, under these accepted definitions of efficiency, from distributing organs in such a fashion.

The other dilemma, alluded to in Chapter 2 of this book, was the circularity of efficiency and rights arguments. As Law and Economics emerged and spread into almost all corners of legal doctrine and interpretation, it brought with it a normative belief that the law "should be" efficient. It should, in other words, maximize a society's resources and minimize its waste.

Upon reflection, this is a rather fascinating viewpoint. There are some who have gone so far as to say this is not only how it "should be", but is, in fact, how it *naturally* is (see Tejani 2021; Wright 2003). Richard Posner, writing in the 1970s, in a time when Law and Economics was still emerging, wrote that the entire common-law tradition follows a pattern of development from less to more efficient (1973). He said that judges and juries have meted out justice over the last several centuries increasingly as if to represent a widespread cultural view that resources are scarce and should be used wisely (1973). It is no coincidence that this has an *evolutionary* ring to it; it suggests that the common-law tradition, like science or politics, "naturally" evolves toward higher states of fairness, transparency, and effectiveness by increasingly embracing rules and outcomes that prioritize efficiency. But, as we know from other domains, this is a suggestion that can never be accurately assessed.

An example of how all this plays out in the real world might go as follows. Say, for instance, that under a certain regime of legal rules, rent controls perhaps, property values in a given area were artificially depressed—held to a level below what would otherwise obtain or what would otherwise encourage owners to consider selling. Then assume that the city or local government is considering whether or not to lift the rent-control law allowing owners to exact higher income for what they own, and to command higher prices from selling their properties in the neighborhood. From the perspective of the real-estate market, the later legal reform might be considered more "efficient": it would permit the existing properties to flow into the hands of those buyers who would value them at their highest level.

What's interesting about this hypothetical is not what it says but what it leaves out. To that end, some (Mercuro and Medema 1997, 120) would respond that the above definition of "efficiency" is specific to a system in which the landowners' rights matter most, above all. In other words, if we prioritize accurate pricing as a measure of efficiency, and if we define accuracy based on the highest valuation, then the market is made more efficient by lifting controls. But if doing so will displace dozens, hundreds, or thousands or residents renting in this area, then it remains to be considered whether and how much the rights of those residents matter in an assessment of market efficiency here. In many cases, "efficiency" has been used as a standard by which to allocate and prioritize competing rights. But for the reason just explained, this has the problem of circularity; if one cannot determine efficiency except with respect to a certain order of rights, then one cannot determine rights based solely on aspirations toward efficiency.

This was captured well by the disciplinary economists Nicholas Mercuro and Steven Medema:

> Because efficiency is a function of rights, and not the other way around, it is circular to maintain that efficiency alone can determine rights. Since costs, prices, outputs, wealth, and so on are derivative of a particular right structure, so too are cost minimization, value of output maximization, and wealth maximization. Different specifications of rights will lead to different (and economically non-comparable) minimizing and maximizing valuations.
>
> (Mercuro and Medema 1997, 118)

Slowness to recognize this may be part and parcel of what Daniel Bell once called the "cult of efficiency" (quoted in Duxbury 1995, 368). This phrase captures a tendency, already evident in mid-century America, toward economic and bureaucratic rationality as *ends in themselves*. This approach came to permeate Western industry in the postwar period and supported unprecedented economic expansion during this time. But it muted more complicated questions about social policy—particularly the ethical questions about what higher sense of "right versus wrong" should be served by the heightened efficiencies achieved through managerial, industrial, and legal innovations.

For Law and Economics, the implication of this slowness is stark. For example, Calabresi has emphatically written that it omits some very significant choices about "taste" lurking behind many lawyer-economist claims about how the world does or should operate (Calabresi 2016, 147–53). In the example above, this would mean the preference for landowner rights to attain maximum property value outweighing tenant rights to affordable housing. To state this preference up front in a public lecture or written article would be one thing, but to proceed "as if" it is not a preference at all and rather part of a natural order of things is something entirely different. But indeed, it may not matter if one speaks only to like-minded observers.

Another example of these limitations lie in the evolving definitions of "efficiency" used by lawyer-economists over time. "Pareto efficiency" describes a distributional scenario in which no additional adjustment or reallocation would make a member of a group or system better off without simultaneously making another worse off. The best distribution prior to that reversal is "optimal"; however, as there can be multiple such positions, the lawyer-economists today speak of the "Pareto frontier", which describes the wider set of ultimately optimal distributions.

For many years, lawyer-economists took Pareto optimality to be the very definition of efficiency by which laws, policies, regulations, should be evaluated normatively—that is to say, assessed for their costs and benefits. But critics began to point out a certain flaw in this account of efficiency: namely, it did not consider transactions *among* members of a community to offset the costs imposed by one party's improvement upon another. So, for instance, a wealthy, absentee landowner who wished to lease part of his property to a rubber-recycling business would cause certain harm to the neighbors; they would experience the noise, noxious fumes, and groundwater pollution resulting from a rubber incinerator, while their neighbor experienced the added monetary benefit of commercial or industrial rents. Simple Pareto optimality would ask whether allowing the factory would, comparing costs and benefits to the individual and community, make the neighbor worse off. In this case, it would rule out the factory as a net-negative use of the community's land, air, and water. For economists, this conclusion could be satisfactory. But for lawyers, whose job it often is to find compromise between divergent interests, it leaves much on the table.

Two criticisms of Pareto optimality thus emerged. One of them says that it is largely irrelevant: that most systems already sit at the Pareto frontier just by virtue of simple market equilibria (Calabresi 2016, 147). Another says that people (and their attorneys) don't simply just walk away from harm-causing activities that might benefit them or their clients personally. Instead, people bargain. The landowner beneficiary of the rubber factory above might offer to pay a monthly or annual fee or honorarium to the neighbor as an incentive to continually allow factory operations, and as compensation for the burdens placed on them. Indeed, the landowner, who would know exactly how much there is to *gain* from the operation, would be well positioned to assess whether the benefit from that outweighs the cost of compensating the neighbor and decide accordingly. If so, then the market, comprised of hundreds or thousands of similar micro-decisions, would naturally reach a state where aggregated benefits outweighed the costs of aggregated harms. In the late 1930s, Kaldor and Hicks built upon the Pareto concept to say "efficiency" was achieved not when no further improvements could be made without making someone worse off but when no further improvements could be made to an economic distribution with the requirement that winners could compensate losers *without* making everyone worse off in the end. In other words, it would be efficient if the new distribution of resources—for instance granting them (e.g., land, air, water) to the landowner for "use" in a rubber-mill operation—it generated were sufficient to both enrich the landowner *and* pay for his neighbors' losses.

It has been long believed that this form of efficiency better captures the collective *social* costs and benefits of a distributive decision and its outcome. But it, too, has come under fire. The majority of Law and Economics work using Kaldor–Hicks efficiency inputs a potential legal solution into an economic calculation to make what is essentially an ethical decision. Here, the legal solution is hypothetical compensatory justice, or damages to be more concrete. The only lawful way to require compensation for one's actions in our system is through the law; a lawsuit can pursue and enforce a court judgment against a polluter, or it can compel enforcement of a regulation and fine on the part of a government agency such as the Environmental Protection Agency (E.P.A.). With Kaldor–Hicks, economists are primarily interested in the former solution, although both may be relevant, since payment of an E.P.A. fine might be structured and viewed as a form of collective compensation.

But standard Kaldor–Hicks analysis does not require that such compensation ever be actually required or enforced. The model only requires that such compensation be possible—meaning that the new harmful activity be worth it if the beneficiary *were* to pay the neighbors for their trouble. As Zachary Liscow (2018) has written, this approach to efficiency, by far the predominant one among lawyer-economists for decades, has been damaging for distributive justice in the United States. Indeed, one must ask, if mandatory compensation is a variable in assessing a decision—about potentially life-altering distributional justice—then why make actual compensation optional?

The answer has to do with the hidden, but all-important role, "society" is playing in these analyses—which are framed as purely economic but which are not. In other words, the above definitions define "efficiency" as maximizing resources in a closed system through actions where either total wealth in the system is increased (Pareto), or where total wealth is increased *and* the individual beneficiaries could compensate any individual victims (Kaldor–Hicks). In either case, social utility is deemed to be served or improved if the assessment criteria are met. But, as I asked in the introductory chapter, what is "society" and what kind of work is that concept doing here?

For sociologists and anthropologists, "society" implies a few key things worth specifying. It suggests first of all *relationships*—not just a couple of relationships, but webs of relationships layered over one another between individuals, between individuals and groups, and among groups. At base, we might think of the way in the Western world our social lives occur among friends and families: those friends and families sit in and transcend neighborhoods, those neighborhoods comprise communities, and communities combine to form towns. Two disparate communities are often required to agree or compromise before any decisions can be made at the level of town government. But none of these "layers" can really exist without the others. And yet, no one plans, designs, and forms them deliberately. They just emerge in and through the many relationships that define them. Second, "society" implies shared *symbolic systems*—a phrase that includes culture, language, and to some extent "values". The belief is that while all humans organize themselves into societies, what distinguishes two or more societies is that they may speak in different languages, utilize different body language, or believe and apply different sets of morals to solving difficult problems. The implications of "society" go much further than just relationships and symbolic systems, but I raise only these two characteristics to ask where, in turn, they leave economics, and thus the definitions of efficiency proffered above.

An action raises social utility if it increases wealth in the society based on either Pareto or Kaldor–Hicks analysis. But how do we know whether two legal actors, one the beneficiary of factory pollution and the other the victim, are in the same "society"? With just the two criteria listed above, we have to ask whether they share a relationship of any kind, and whether they do so with any kind of meaningful shared symbolic system. For two neighbors across an adjoining fence, it might be easy to assume "yes" to both questions: the chances are great (though far from certain) that they have met and that they speak a similar language. But for two actors not joined by a property boundary, nor even the same street or subdivision, it gets trickier. Is an absentee factory owner in the same "society" as low-income residents of the adjacent, downwind community? Would they see one another passing on the street, and would they give each other a greeting in the same language if so? These may seem ancillary to the question of economic cost and benefit in the community, but the use of "social utility" as a measure for right *vs.* wrong actions already made them important. In other words, how can we conclude an economic action benefits a society "as a whole" if we spend no time considering the boundaries of that society in the first place?

As already indicated, many of the influential ideas in Law and Economics make no mention of this nuance, and instead they proceed from an assumption that there just are "societies" which we are all part of today. This assumed *society* tends to sound most like "country" or "nation", but it is rarely specified in these manners. The point in saying all of this is that Law and Economics, while trying to contain or evade complicated questions about culture and society, in fact leaves open-ended and unexamined the way that these color its analyses. Or, to put it differently, economic life cannot be treated as separate and outside of social life; it can, rather, only be understood as *embedded* in it (Tejani 2018).

The View from Outside: Critiques

As with any other investigation, an effort to understand Law and Economics requires both a deeper look inside the discipline *and* a move outward to view the community and movement in a broader perspective. As already mentioned, Law and Economics has proven to be one of the most dominant subfields in the study of law over the past several decades. Looking solely at the number of law-school faculty hires from economics over that period, no other interdisciplinary subfield comes close in numbers and, by implication, therefore, influence. This comes, again by implication, at the exclusion of other law-related social science fields. For this reason, scholars in those neighboring fields have had much to say about the "economization" of law and law school faculties. On the one hand, there is much to be learned from these criticisms. On the other hand, one must be mindful of misunderstandings and information deficiencies whenever outsider accounts of a group or community are used as data about it.

In this case, the general tenor of outsider accounts from the social sciences has been critical. Among sociologists and anthropologists especially—and among political scientists and historians to a lesser degree—the general concern is that Law and Economics promotes a view of the law as merely an instrument of economic growth. This may seem innocuous at first, but consider historic legal victories that have prioritized civil or human rights in the past. Such decisions were rooted in definitions of justice that were largely "social" by nature. They embraced definitions of "society" that are about relationships, cultural integration, and interlocking duties people have with one another in communities. Law and Economics, meanwhile, has either tended to view "society" as a web of economic transactions or as "deals" among individual actors acting in their own interest. There is, in other words, no freestanding "society"; there are only individuals who form allegiances and behavioral patterns to maximize self-interest. Society, in other words, is merely a byproduct of economic activity. This view, in turn, forces lawyer-economists to explain away social and cultural phenomena—such as altruism or acting in others' best interest—as either "irrational" or "boundedly rational". In his history of American legal thought, British scholar Neil Duxbury terms this reductionism "economic imperialism" (Duxbury 1995, 379). It describes the notion that a broad spectrum of human activity can (and indeed must) be understood through the lens of economics. For law, this has very deep implications. As Richard Posner has said in various ways, under a Law and Economics approach the very definition of *justice* is "economic efficiency" (1981).

This reduction of human behavior and ethics—debates over right versus wrong—has irked sociologists and anthropologists for some time.

They view it as part of the wider trend in politics, policy, and government administration known as *neoliberalism*. Neoliberalism has come to mean an ideological position wherein economic freedom and citizenship are the primary measure of social and political progress. Under this view, communities that are dependent on government assistance (even for clear reasons of historical specificity, for instance slavery), are not truly free, and are not realizing their human potential. Indeed, neoliberal thought associates most forms of government or public assistance with "socialism"—a term loosely used to describe economic and political systems using "command structures" such as government planning or price controls. One of the leading proponents of this ideology was U.S. President Ronald Reagan. A close adherent of Milton Friedman's economic worldview, and of Ayn Rand's individualist philosophy, Reagan systematically dismantled social welfare programs, trade union protections, and public utilities in the United States under the banner of Cold War anti-communism (Harvey 2007; Ong 2006). While this was happening, a similar movement was taking place in the United Kingdom under Prime Minister Margaret Thatcher. Today, Reagan and Thatcher are considered the faces of neoliberalism in national policy and international relations.

But the neoliberal wave, it must be stressed, is far more than a governmental or international movement. What makes it truly remarkable are the many ways in which it was translated, circulated, and embraced by ordinary people in everyday domestic life. In the realm of higher education and professional life, this could be seen in the rapid rise of business school teaching and study in the West. No longer a site for "liberal education" in the classic subjects such as rhetoric and philosophy, universities saw the influx of more and more students looking for marketable skills that would earn them a well-paid job upon graduation, and income levels that would sustain the increasingly high sticker price of Western higher education. As this occurred, a natural credentials "arms race" emerged, making master's degrees the new baccalaureate and sparking an explosion in M.B.A. programs. The creation of a new professional class of M.B.A. graduates in turn brought an influx of business trainees in a new array of industries including healthcare and higher education. This final development saw a stricter cost–benefit approach imported into important caregiving and knowledge-producing fields, resulting in widespread budget-cutting, reduction in unprofitable programs, and, most importantly, a turn to private-sector sources for funding such as corporations, financial firms, and high-net-worth individuals.

Sociologists and anthropologists have been widely critical of this neoliberal turn. It runs counter to many of the foundational assumptions and beliefs of most social sciences. First, by holding that society is merely a group of individuals with no unique qualities of its own, it denies the underlying view in sociology and anthropology traceable to the French theorist Emile Durkheim that individuals *realize* their sense of self through group belonging and participation. Imagine, for example, trying to explain who you are without reference to your family, your neighborhood, or your city. The famous adage that "no man (or woman) is an island" is instructive here. Social scientists since Durkheim have been well aware of this and study the numerous ways in which it proves true. Second, the more normative approach of neoliberalism says that because society is just individuals, then individuals are solely responsible for their own fate within society. If you are wealthy, that is because you or someone connected to you worked very hard or creatively as an individual. They created "value" and were empowered to profit from that as individuals. If you are poor, that is because you or someone in your ancestry made bad choices. Because of this view, neoliberalism envisions a world in which the state or the government provides minimal public benefits such as income assistance, free healthcare, or free childcare to those in need. In some cases, it pushes those individuals to find work (or more work, given the low minimum wage in many countries) on the belief that the market will best handle their income needs.

These two facets of the neoliberal wave, the one descriptive and the other normative, are two of the main reasons why sociologists and anthropologists have not embraced most of what the lawyer-economists have been saying about law in society for the past six decades. For them, law is, and should be, a tool for pursuing greater equity in society. On the far extreme side sit those who would prefer a command economy where prices and income levels could be established by a central body—an approach often called socialism by those who dislike it. On the near side, sit those who would accept the current economic system provided that the law can do more to offset the gross inequalities that result. Today, for example, the wealthiest ten percent in the United States control 70 percent of the nation's wealth (Siripurapu 2022). This is a concentration greater than at any previous time since the Great Depression. This wealth inequality is often referred to as a problem of *distributive justice*. If justice is the concept of finding the right solutions where wrongs have been committed, distributive justice is the application of such solutions specifically where wealth and income inequalities have resulted from prior action or inaction. Not everyone believes distributive justice should be the goal of law; lawyer-economists were often the most vocal in saying this. As Mercuro and Medema have written, "[A]lthough distribution is often included in the rhetoric of some schools of thought, it is, more often than not, overlooked by much of the work in the economic analysis of law" (1997, 24).

For sociologists and anthropologists, understanding the role of law in creating or supporting inequality has deep roots. The German theorist Max Weber virtually invented modern sociology by developing several sweeping studies of social control in his era (Weber 1958). In much the way Durkheim did, Weber viewed the individual as both empowered and constrained by group membership, but he went further in studying the structures by which human beings organize themselves into groups beyond the family. This led Weber to study modern bureaucracies, religious sects, and professions; from those studies, he concluded that human beings had "rationalized" modern life to such an extent that we are all now—under a capitalist economy and its laws—enabled and constrained by an "iron cage" of rules and processes (Weber 1978). Several of Weber's students went on to refine the sociology of professions; C. Wright Mills, for example, published a seminal study of business and legal professionals in 1951, just at the time that Western post–World War II societies came to idealize the professional class of men working in office jobs while conforming to strict standards of dress, fashion, consumption, and career development—not to mention the gender stereotypes evidently restored since their wartime disruption. In the intervening years, with decolonization and civil rights battles raging around the world, sociology moved toward the study of identity and group mobilization—a sort of turn toward the grassroots and away from organizations of the kind Weber and Mills were interested in. In the 1980s, perhaps because of the neoliberal turn toward individualism—a turn Nancy Fraser has since connected to the aforementioned liberation struggles—sociology experienced a return to interest in organizations in what is now called *neo-institutionalism*. This approach, still very much a dominant school of thought, believes organizations such as corporations, government agencies, and non-profit providers, are themselves grounds for group and individual identity formation and belonging (Powell and DiMaggio 1991). In the study of law, neo-institutionalists have shown the ways in which legal meanings and processes are, in fact, largely the result of organizational culture and behavior. Few examples are as powerful as Lauren Edelman's 2016 book *Working Law*, which showed handily that the civil rights laws of the 1960s and 1970s came to be largely interpreted and applied *through* private corporation human resource departments over the 1980s and 1990s. This theory, which Edelman terms *legal endogeneity*, offers a smart explanation for the interaction between public (e.g., government) and private (e.g., corporate) law in our world.

Perhaps with this understanding in development, Edelman wrote, in her presidential address to the Law and Society Association, that Law and Economics and Law and Society were at a crossroads to begin collaborating to understand the complex connections between law, economics, and social life (Edelman 2004). "The time is ripe", she wrote, "for L&S and L&E to engage in a dialogue that will ultimately enrich our understanding of law and the economy. Ideally, this dialogue will help us move beyond the impasse of the norms-vs.-efficiency debate that too often impedes further discussion" (2004, 183). This call for dialogue went substantially "unanswered", and it still echoes in the space between the two subfields. It is substantially as a response that this book was written.

Meanwhile, in anthropology, the study of law and legal behavior has been similarly isolated from the goings-on of Law and Economics. On the one hand, the anthropological study of law has flourished in its own right. With roots deep in the history of classic anthropology, legal anthropology began with the study of so-called primitive societies and their norm systems (Moore 2005). The reason was simple: Western countries had close contact with these people around the world due to their colonial domination of them. Among others, the French held much of North Africa and East Asia; the British held South Asia, Eastern and Southern Africa, and some of the Middle East and Southeast Asia; and the United States held the territories of indigenous people in North America, Alaska, and the South Pacific. Understanding local customs and rules was a key part of understanding how to control the people of these territories. Whereas scholars, policymakers, and jurists at the time still considered these people lacking in organized "law", the early anthropologists came to show that social norms in these places generally worked like law and were functionally the same thing (Moore 2005). By the late 20th century there was little dispute that non-Western and indigenous societies were absolutely governed by "law", but also that the measure of "law" could not simply be what European and North American jurists practiced it as. With that realization, the anthropology of law turned increasingly back toward Euro-American legal institutions, rules, and processes in both formal (e.g., courtroom) and informal (e.g., church, family) settings. These studies suggested law to be one of a number of expert social fields and provoked anthropologists to want to understand the contours of its character: where did it begin and end, how was expertise reproduced, transmitted, or signaled, and how did individual and group lives get shaped by accessing it?

This made the late 20th-century anthropology of law a close correlative to the anthropology of science. There, great strides had been made in studying biomedical (Dumit 2004), technological (Turkle 1997), and engineering (Gusterson 1996) scientific communities. The French ethnographer Bruno Latour—a founder of actor-network theory in science studies—eventually made the crossover to ethnography of law with a noteworthy field study of the French lawmaking body the *Conseil d'Etat* (Latour 2009). This type of work realizes a connection foreshadowed by Max Weber a century earlier between his studies of bureaucratic life and "science as a vocation" (Weber 1958). Connecting these, already for Weber, was an economic dimension that would get most attention in anthropology with vigorous study and criticism of neoliberalism. Unlike in sociology, where quantitative data still played a major role, in anthropology the fieldwork qualitative methodology meant more and more researchers sought to understand the way neoliberal policies and structures—the ones that said individuals should work for welfare benefits, or developing countries must marketize to receive international aid—were actually lived and experienced by the people most impacted by them. From these studies, two writers stand out as particularly connected to the social study of Law and Economics. The first is Carol Greenhouse for her books *The Paradox of Relevance* (2011) and *Ethnographies of Neoliberalism* (2010). While not unique in their treatment of neoliberal social life and its discontents, Greenhouse (and the ethnographic studies she assembles) offers some of the most lucid descriptions of what market fundamentalism did to the concept of "society" in the West during the 1980s and 1990s. The adoption of neoliberal policies—in other words the adoption of law to support an economic definition of society, as neoliberalism does—shifted the very place of "social life" and any studies of it:

> The fact that relevance was presented as a mediating path in relation to anthropology's internal debates implied that anthropologists had only themselves to blame if the public overwhelmingly communicated through other channels. In retrospect, this accusation misses the mark. It was politics that abandoned society as social—the basis of social security—and failed the people with whom anthropologists most readily identified, that is, minority communities at the social margins.
>
> (Greenhouse 2011, 34)

This thick little passage could serve as an instruction manual for anyone wishing to know what anthropology thinks about Law and Economics. The latter, I have already said, views *economic* activity as the primary measure of social well-being and connectedness. Any extrinsic behavior or symbolic practices—for example, graduation parties—can be explained in relation to some underlying economic function. Anthropologists not only disagree with this premise; they felt, increasingly since the 2000s, that the permeation of economic essentialism it represents is greatly responsible for transforming the contemporary world from a matrix of social connections into a network of economic transactions—in other words, for auguring a crisis of social belonging identifiable in everything from school shootings and healthcare costs to teacher shortages and for-profit prisons.

Secondly, Sally Merry's work on quantification is an anthropologist's perspective on the imperious rise of data collection and processing as the primary means for expertise to understand our world (2016). This work draws upon diverse ethnographic and "documentary" datasets concerning the use of three major indicators in the work of global civil-society programs. These include violence against women, human trafficking, and general human rights abuses (2016). Merry argues that, "despite the value of numbers for exposing problems and tracking their distribution, they provide knowledge that is decontextualized, homogenized, and remote from local systems of meaning" (2016, 3). The implications of this claim, that quantification leads to both clarity and distortion, are stark for Law and Economics. For this subfield, quantification remains the primary basis for scholarly and policy arguments. Even where there have been more qualitative, behavioral studies, they have been designed to improve quantitative understandings about economic activity more so than displace them. For example, Sunstein and Thaler (2009) argue that greater understanding of behavioral choices can support better "choice architecture" on the part of lawmakers, and this is directed at better large-scale macro-level social coercion—for instance, in anti-smoking campaigns or tax policy. Even more starkly, Merry's argument runs directly counter to most empirical Law and Economics that aims to "see through" shifting moral and cultural "beliefs" to get at more objective markers of what people value and to what degree.

Finally, recent developments in economic anthropology have brought that subfield closer to (though not *into*) conversations with Law and Economics. As I have said elsewhere (forthcoming), economic anthropology's renewed interest in theories of "value" has the potential to shed light on an age-old but oft-neglected problem of understanding the values that underpin valuation. David Graeber captures this problem lucidly in his 2001 book:

> There are, one might say, three large streams of thought that converge in the present term. These are: 1. "values" in the sociological sense: conceptions of what is ultimately good, proper, or desirable in human life[;] 2.) "value" in the economic sense: the degree to which objects are desired [... and] 3.) "value" in the linguistic sense [...] simply glossed as "meaningful difference".
>
> (Graeber 2001, 1–2)

Tracing the concept through the writings of Marx, Marcel Mauss, Marvin Harris, and Michael Taussig among others, Graeber writes that social researchers have used "value" interchangeably between the moral, economistic, and linguistic meanings of the term, and that attempts to parse the boundaries between each have largely been abandoned. He concludes that the limitations of delineating those boundaries are very telling, and that today's value theory should attend to how and why the term can mean all three things, often at once (2001).

Conclusion

The final pages here point to a deficit in legal-economic thought concerning the concept of value, as well to a normative suggestion that Law and Economics and sociologists and anthropologists of law—sociolegal scholars, as they are known collectively—might approach more refined models of value if they could converse and collaborate at greater levels than currently visible. The establishment of any new school of thought, if that is what this means, is complicated and time-consuming. As with Behavioral Law and Economics, or the underlying rise of Law and Economics itself, this takes resources, work, and leadership that is presently lacking. Unlike these fields, however, there are more concrete historical roadblocks to collaboration that would need transcending.

As the brief history in Chapter 2 reveals, Law and Economics began as a counter-movement to "push back" influences of New Deal social welfare and Civil Rights–era social justice most clearly manifested in the Critical Legal Studies (C.L.S.) movement in U.S. law schools. Law and Economics received much of its early financial support specifically to attempt to resist C.L.S. (Teles 2008, 192). C.L.S. evolved into the contemporary Law and Society community, and Law and Society has not easily forgotten the early and ongoing challenges. Looking at the number of law-school faculty hires in both fields over the last several decades, it would appear Law and Economics won out (McCrary et al. 2016, 556). Moreover, among contemporary scholars of Law and Society, Law and Economics has been greatly responsible for the advent of neoliberal policies and the philosophies underpinning them. So, there are those in both camps who might view cooperation today as a betrayal. Relatedly, there are some deep methodological differences separating these fields—especially surrounding the basic concept of "society". For lawyer-economists, society is usually a sum total of individuals and their preferences (Shavell 2003), whereas for sociolegal experts (following in the tradition of Emile Durkheim) (2001, 2014) society is its own unique thing—greater than the sum of its parts. This difference, too, makes cooperation seem treasonous to some.

And yet, despite the nomenclatures applied to academic disciplines and publication genres, no one group of experts possesses a monopoly on research questions—only, if at all, on methods of investigation. It is clear that Law and Economics and Sociolegal studies have been approaching many of the same questions—or assuming answers to them—using different and oftentimes complementary methods. The opening chapter of this book asked the reader to reflect on a series of such questions throughout. They were: What is society? What is culture? What does it mean to be rational? What is utility and what is freedom? None of these can remotely be answered by Law and Economics alone. The way forward, therefore, requires an approach we might call "Critical Law and Economics". Critical Law and Economics takes the conventional criticisms of Law and Economics that emerged from the interpretive social sciences and humanities and, rather than dismiss the latter as ill-founded, seeks to address the significant rhetorical gaps highlighted by the several questions raised at the outset and above. It is therefore epistemologically (e.g., "how we know what we know") critical but descriptively sympathetic. It applies "our" descriptive tools to illuminate areas left obscured and assumed away by first-, second-, and third-wave lawyer-economists. The purpose, make no mistake, is not to help "confirm" or reify normative suggestions—such as that adjudication should mimic market transactions—that Law and Economics has offered. It is to test and challenge those assertions using the strongest version of Law and Economics we can contend with.

To that effect, *society* is more than the net total of individuals and their preferences: it consists of the relationships people are born into, socialized by, and motivated to forge. Sometimes those relationships are intended for financial gain, but oftentimes they are for the sake of connection alone and, as such, may run counter to economic interest. *Culture*, we also know, is more than simply a batch of behavioral side constraints to economic activity. Certainly, it can help explain why and how some place social connections above economic interests, but it also consists of *all* the expressive raw materials from which human thought and emotion are conveyed or memorialized. Attempts to generalize from monocultural economic behavior without acknowledgment of the actual complexity manifested in global, cross-cultural contexts—for example, mysterious differences in litigation settlement rates in transnational perspective—are therefore ostensibly superficial and vague. Likewise, *rationality* is difficult to generalize except in very loose form, and conforms to different norms depending on social and cultural contexts. It is only "bounded"—as per Behavioral Law and Economics—in the sense of clinical research settings, and it is rather "contextual" or "situated" by almost all other social science or humanities accounts. Similarly, *utility*, or the sense of pleasure derived from any act, will be equally contextual or situated; it is, therefore, mostly generalizable at high levels of abstraction, and to know any more about this, on-ground fieldwork studies would be needed as to how people actually use and feel about things. And finally, we glean from social sciences and humanities—to the potential benefit of lawyer-economists—that *freedom* is an ever-evolving, relative, and historically embedded notion not to be assumed fixed and serviced by policies that appear to eliminate the state from daily life. In certain obvious contexts, the state has been, for some, the only guarantor of human freedom; in others, there is no other party capable of accurately assessing and remedying problems of distributive justice in society—even if imperfectly. Recognition and further pursuit of these nuances will be, I maintain, essential for lawyer-economists to maintain relevance in our world of building inequalities.

Law and Economics may not be "new", but it constitutes a "new trajectory in law", thanks to the promise it continues to hold out for solving large societal problems. This book has examined its key ideas, its origins, and its global itinerary, in part to reveal that Law and Economics has, at certain moments, contributed to the very problems it now hopes to resolve. But, in doing so, it has also revealed substantial room for intellectual bridge-building—with Sociolegal scholars especially—to sharpen its perspective on a world it has already changed.

References

Calabresi, Guido, and Douglas A. Melamed. 1972. "Property Rules, Liability Rules, and Inalienability: One View of the Cathedral." *Harvard Law Review* 85 (6): 1089–1128.

Calabresi, Guido. 2016. *The Future of Law and Economics.* New Haven, CT: Yale University Press.

Cass, Sunstein, and Richard Thaler. 2009. *Nudge: Improving Decisions About Health, Wealth, and Happiness.* New York: Penguin Books.

Dumit, Joseph. 2004. *Picturing Personhood Brain Scans and Biomedical Identity.* Princeton, NJ: Princeton University Press.

Durkheim, Emile. 2001 [1912]. *The Elementary Forms of Religious Life.* Oxford: Oxford University Press.

Durkheim, Emile. 2014 [1893]. *The Division of Labor in Society.* New York: The Free Press.

Duxbury, Neil. 1995. *Patterns of American Jurisprudence.* Oxford: Oxford University Press.

Edelman, Lauren. 2004. "Rivers of Law and Contested Terrain: A Law and Society Approach to Economic Rationality." *Law and Society Review* 38 (2): 181–198.

Edelman, Lauren. 2016. *Working Law: Courts, Corporations, and Symbolic Civil Rights*, Chicago, IL: University of Chicago Press.

Graeber, David. 2001. *Toward an Anthropological Theory of Value.* New York: Palgrave-MacMillan.

Greenhouse, Carol J. ed. 2010. *Ethnographies of Neoliberalism.* Philadelphia, PA: University of Pennsylvania Press.

Greenhouse, Carol J. 2011. *The Paradox of Relevance.* Philadelphia, PA: University of Pennsylvania Press.

Gusterson, Hugh. 1996. *Nuclear Rites: A Weapons Laboratory at the End of the Cold War.* Berkeley, CA: University of California Press.

Harvey, David. 2007. *A Brief History of Neoliberalism*. Oxford and New York: Oxford University Press.

Latour, Bruno. 2009. *Making Law: An Ethnography of the Conseil D'Etat*. Cambridge: Polity.

Liscow, Zachary. 2018. "Is Efficiency Biased?" *University of Chicago Law Review* 85: 1649–1718.

Mercuro, Nicholas, and Steven Medema. 1997. *Economics and the Law: From Posner to Post-Modernism and Beyond*. Princeton, NJ: Princeton University Press.

Merry, Sally Engle. 2016. *The Seductions of Quantification: Measuring Human Rights, Gender Violence, and Sex Trafficking*. Chicago, IL: University of Chicago.

McCrary, Justin, Joy Milligan, and James Phillips. 2016. "The Ph.D. Rises in American law schools, 1960–2011: What does it Mean for Legal Education?" *Journal of Legal Education* 65(3): 543– 579.

Moore, Sally Falk. 2005. "General Introduction." In Sally Falk Moore ed. *Law and Anthropology: A Reader*. Oxford: Blackwell Publishing, 1–5.

Ong, Aihwa. 2006. *Neoliberalism as Exception: Mutations in Citizenship and Sovereignty*. Durham, NC: Duke University Press.

Powell, Walter W., and Paul J. DiMaggio. 1991. *The New Institutionalism in Organizational Analysis*. Chicago, IL: University of Chicago Press.

Posner, Richard. 1973. *The Economic Analysis of Law*. New York: Aspen Publishers.

Posner, Richard 1981. *The Economics of Justice*. Cambridge, MA: Harvard University Press.

Shavell, Steve. 2003. "Economic Analysis of Welfare Economics, Morality and the Law." NBER Working Paper No. 9700, May 2003.

Siripurapu, Anshu. 2022. "The U.S. Inequality Debate." Council on Foreign Relations, https://www.cfr.org/backgrounder/us-inequality-debate. Accessed May 15, 2023.

Teles, Steven M. 2008. *The Rise of the Conservative Legal Movement*. Princeton, NJ: Princeton University Press.

Tejani, Riaz. 2021. "The Life of Transplants: Why Law and Economics Has Succeeded Where Legal Anthropology Has Not." *Alabama Law Review* 73 (4): 733–752.

Tejani, Riaz. 2018. "A Working Class Profession: Opportunism and Diversity in U.S. Law." *Dialectical Anthropology* 42 (2): 131–148.

Turkle, Sherry. 1997. *Life on the Screen: Identity in the Age of the Internet*. New York: Simon and Schuster.

Weber, Max. 1958. *From Max Weber: Essays in Sociology*. Oxford: Oxford University Press.

Weber, Max. 1978. *Economy and Society: An Outline of Interpretive Sociology*. Berkeley, CA: University of California Press, 220–221.

Wright, Richard. 2003. "Hand, Posner, and the Myth of the "Hand Formula."" *Theoretical Inquiries in Law* 4(1): 145–274.

Index

For Product Safety Concerns and Information please contact our EU
representative GPSR@taylorandfrancis.com
Taylor & Francis Verlag GmbH, Kaufingerstraße 24, 80331 München, Germany